Yale Studies in English, 179

Form and Transformation
in Music and Poetry of the
English Renaissance

by Paula Johnson

New Haven and London: Yale University Press, 1972

Library of Congress catalog card number: 72–75197
International standard book number: 0–300–01544–5

Designed by John O. C. McCrillis
and set in Baskerville type.
Printed in the United States of America by
The Colonial Press Inc., Clinton, Massachusetts.

Published in Great Britain, Europe, and Africa by
Yale University Press, Ltd., London.
Distributed in Canada by McGill-Queen's University Press, Montreal;
in Latin America by Kaiman & Polon, Inc., New York City; in Australasia
and Southeast Asia by John Wiley & Sons Australasia Pty. Ltd., Sydney;
in India by UBS Publishers' Distributors Pvt., Ltd., Delhi;
in Japan by John Weatherhill, Inc., Tokyo.

For Muriel

. . . the fire and the rose are one.

Contents

Acknowledgments

It was my good fortune to be permitted to write as a dissertation the study that I had been thinking toward for some years. My first interest in comparisons between the arts I owe to Professor Imanuel Willheim of the Hartt College of Music, whose lively and wide-ranging seminar made me aware of the promises and problems of *geistesgeschichte*. My debts to other teachers, friends, and writers are innumerable; I should like to thank especially William Waite and Eugene Waith for their helpful comments on parts of the manuscript; Richard Sylvester for his guidance in preparing the whole for publication; and above all, Marie Borroff, for her encouragement and acute criticism of the work-in-progress. My husband prepared an invaluable file of the relevant recorded music; for that and for his unfailing patience, I am permanently grateful.

In its initial form, as a doctoral dissertation presented to the Yale Graduate School, this book received the John Addison Porter Prize in 1969.

1

Serial Art: Problems and Assumptions

The old distinction, made in its clearest form by Lessing in the
Laokoön, between temporal and spatial arts is beginning to be
broken down. Writers like Gombrich suggest a temporal dimension for pictures, and others like Zuckerkandl insist upon
a spatial dimension for music; Joseph Frank, in an influential
essay, has defined what he calls "spatial form" in modern literature.[1] It is evident that we can no longer take quite for
granted Lessing's simple division of the arts into those that like
painting or sculpture can be comprehended in a moment, and
those that like music and poetry require for their comprehension an extended period of time. And it is not just in experimental modern works that the division seems no longer useful;
it seems never to have held for the dance, and still less for even
the most primitive of motion pictures. But in spite of all this,
there does seem to be some basic difference between those arts
that do and those that do not determine the sequential order
of their own apprehension.[2] No matter how "open" a musical
work of Stockhausen or of Cage may be, the listener still cannot choose to have its sounds presented to him in any other
order than that in which they are in fact presented. It is primarily, I suppose, a question of the listener's willingness to surrender his expectations to the fact of that order.

In literature the convention of reading from left to right will

1. E. H. Gombrich, "Moment and Movement in Art," *Journal of the
Warburg and Courtauld Institute* 27 (1964): 293–306; Victor Zuckerkandl,
Sound and Symbol: Music and the External World; Joseph Frank, "Spatial
Form in Modern Literature," in *The Widening Gyre*, pp. 3–62.
2. See Stephen C. Pepper, *The Basis of Criticism in the Arts*, pp. 158–59.

inevitably affect the order of a reader's experience, whether or
not he begins a book at the beginning, goes on to the end, and
then stops. And even in musical compositions where the musician looking at a specially designed score must determine for
himself where to begin and how to proceed, once he has done
so, the order he produces becomes in turn the order he perceives, and that order (however radically it may seem to differ
from conventional notions of musical form) will be for him
as for a passive audience the sequence in which elements *must*
be realized because they *are* so realized. It is not improper,
then, to speak of the sequence as fixed, since fixed sequence
characterizes our experience of music and of poetry. Although
the experience of sequence implies duration, it does not necessarily imply "time" or "space" in either Lessing's or Frank's
sense; we may therefore discard these categories, and deal with
the sequences as they occur. With this in mind, Susanne Langer
suggested the adjective "occurrent" instead of "temporal"; but
I think the simplest way to refer to arts whose perception is
sequentially fixed is to call them *serial* arts, and the form that
is thus produced, serial form.[3]

When we turn to older works, the problem of serial form
becomes, if not simpler, at any rate more familiar. Even if we
begin rereading *King Lear* with the storm on the heath, then
skip back to the first scene, then on to Lear's reconciliation
with Cordelia, this wresting of the sequence of events in our
actual experience does not substantially affect our recognition
that there is a fixed sequence determined by the poet, in terms
of which we interpret the most desultory actual process of reading. The same rule would hold for a singer practicing a non-
strophic song: no matter at what point a given rehearsal begins and no matter which sections require working over, it will
still be recognized that the composer (and of course the poet)
has determined the particular sequence that gives the song its

3. An example of the confusion to which the word "temporal" may lend
itself is Joan Stambaugh, "Music as a Temporal Form," *Journal of Philosophy* 61 (1964): 265–80. For the term "occurrent" see Susanne K. Langer,
Feeling and Form, p. 121.

form and identity. Any playgoer, any reader, any listener will understand these forms as forms.

Even though it may take some time to apprehend a painting, the painting is all there all the time. But a song or play or poem is not all there all the time; it happens to us bit by bit. Psychologists have done research and experimentation to ascertain how we perceive objects that are presented to us all at once; but what of objects that are presented piecemeal? How is it that we make out an organized "shape" in objects so presented? How can there be such a thing as serial form? The charges made by contemporary composers that the need to perceive form in music is a kind of escapism[4] do scant justice to the mystery of how we managed ever to perceive the forms in the first place. It seems in fact much easier to understand how we can surrender ourselves to "indeterminacy" than to account for our not doing so. Unfortunately, it is not only the avant-garde musicians (to whom we must allow the right of beginning wherever it seems good to them) who take the apprehension of serial form for granted; but so too do the psychologists, for the most part; and so, almost universally, do critics of both music and literature. Time in art is normally treated as a philosophical problem, part of the larger inquiry into the nature of time and space prompted by the discoveries of modern physics.[5] But such inquiry is only indirectly helpful to the concrete, practical study of our experience of serial form. In the absence of developed research that might give a firm foundation for the attempt to understand this neglected phenomenon, we shall have to proceed syncretically, taking advantage of the investigations and speculations in different fields that make contact with our problem from their various directions.

4. See Van Meter Ames, "What Is Music?" *Journal of Aesthetics and Art Criticism* 26 (1967): 241–49.

5. See, besides the works already cited, Patricia Carpenter, "Musical Form Regained," *Journal of Philosophy* 62 (1965): 36–48; Ida Fasel, "Spatial Form and Spatial Time," *Western Humanities Review* 16 (1962): 223–34; J. T. Fraser, ed., *The Voices of Time,* especially the essay by Walther Dürr, "Rhythm in Music: A Formal Scaffolding of Time," pp. 180–200; Jacques Maritain, *Creative Intuition in Art and Poetry.*

One of these is the study of changes in artistic style, especially when such study relates two or more arts to each other.
Among the earliest and best of these period studies is Wölfflin's
Principles of Art History, which proposes five polar dimensions
to characterize the difference between Renaissance and baroque
style in the visual arts. Wölfflin, although he did not question
the basic fact of form perception, contributed to its recognition
by setting up ways of identifying its types, especially in his
categories of open versus closed form and multiple versus unified unity. Other scholars have taken up Wölfflin's suggestions
and tried to extend his method to literature;[6] these attempts
are often interesting, but they encounter a number of difficulties. The problem of defining terms is the most pervasive of
these, along with too heavy a reliance on the critic's own individual impressions, and the very questionable assumption that
there are such things as "periods" to be described.[7] From our
present viewpoint, the most serious deficiency in the period
studies is their consistent failure to examine the nature of the
perception that allows the critic to make a period study in the
first place. It is not only the often too facile drawing of analogies between "spatial" and "temporal" arts that is the problem
here,[8] but the lack of investigation into the temporal forms
themselves. But, again from our present viewpoint, the very
existence of period studies testifies to the almost automatic,
subjectively convincing quality of the perception of serial

6. E.g. Helmut Hatzfeld, *Literature through Art*; Wylie Sypher, *Four
Stages of Renaissance Style*; Imbrie Buffum, *Agrippa d'Aubigne's "Les
Tragiques."*

7. The period theory has been honored by much thoughtful opposition,
e.g. Arthur O. Lovejoy, "On the Discrimination of Romanticisms," in
Essays in the History of Ideas, pp. 228–53; James Mark, "The Uses of the
Term 'Baroque,'" *Modern Language Review* 33 (1938): 547–63; René
Wellek, *Concepts of Criticism;* Alden Buker, "The Baroque S-T-O-R-M:
A Study in the Limits of the Culture-Epoch Theory," *Journal of Aesthetics
and Art Criticism* 22 (1964): 303–13.

8. See René Wellek, "The Parallelism between Literature and the Arts,"
in *English Institute Annual, 1941*; and Walter Sutton, "The Literary Image and the Reader: A Consideration of the Theory of Spatial Form,"
Journal of Aesthetics and Art Criticism 16 (1957): 112–23.

forms; and here and there, since this is also to be in its way a period study, their suggestions may turn out to confirm conclusions reached from a different angle.

In the more limited field of specifically literary criticism, the most interesting recent attempt to theorize in terms of whole forms is Northrop Frye's *Anatomy of Criticism.* Frye's technique of standing off from literary works in order to abstract the constant ways of organizing plots is of course open to the charge of reductionism; but it remains true that this middle distance provides a useful temporary stance, and that the suppression of detail can show up formal characteristics well worth our recognition.[9] If we are to examine the perception of literary form, it will be imperative to do so from afar as well as close up. Professor Frye, however, has not been primarily concerned with literary perception as I am trying to understand it; he concentrates on what goes on in what is being read, rather than on what goes on in the reader. Although a rigid distinction between subject and object does not seem to me very fruitful for this investigation, it is possible to put the emphasis one way or the other. In literature it has very rarely been put on the subject: I. A. Richards did so, as have a few psychoanalytically oriented critics like Simon Lesser and Norman Holland; and from yet another viewpoint, Louise Rosenblatt,[10] but none of these has explored the cognitive response to poetry in much detail. Such exploration requires whatever help we can get from the psychologists; if carried out systematically it may indicate a psychology of criticism, as opposed to the more usual psychologies of authors and of fictive characters.

These considerations, then, bring us to the more general question of the relations between literature and psychology, and (since my main inquiry regards serial, not just literary

9. Cf. I. A. Richards, *Practical Criticism,* p. 40.

10. Simon O. Lesser, *Fiction and the Unconscious;* Norman Holland, *The Dynamics of Literary Response;* Louise M. Rosenblatt, "Towards a Transactional Theory of Reading," *Journal of Reading Behavior* 1 (1969): 31–50.

form) to the psychology of music. The two arts have made contact with psychology at different points. For literature, the medium of relationship has most often been Freud, who made some literary investigations himself, and who provided terms for analyses of content. The bias of literary psychology has therefore been almost exclusively psychoanalytic;[11] far less has been done between literature and other branchs of psychology. A distinguished exception was Kenneth Burke (to some of whose formulations my own are deeply indebted), but even Burke did not draw on psychology as a discipline so much as on his own highly discriminating responses.[12] It seems that the psychology of conscious processes—academic as differentiated from clinical investigations—has scarcely come to the attention of literary critics. Perhaps this is because we laymen tend to associate academic psychology with the study of animal behavior and intelligence tests, or because its research sticks to experimentally verifiable terms not easily transferred to literary interests; in any case, the separation between the two fields is virtually complete.

The situation in regard to music is different and somewhat more encouraging. This field, the psychology of music, is less apt to be familiar to students of literature, so I shall summarize what seem the most pertinent developments. Experimental investigations carried out by Carl Seashore in the 1930s were "based upon the analysis of the musical medium—the physical sound." Seashore believed that "the central problem in the psychology of music is the description and explanation of the musical creation—the actual music—regarded as the stimulus for arousing musical feeling." [13] Since that stimulus is physical sound, the experimental evidence that Seashore collected has

11. The history of this relationship has been conveniently outlined by Paul C. Obler, "Psychology and Literary Criticism: A Summary and Critique," *Literature and Psychology* 8 (1958): 50–59; Claudia Morrison has discussed it in detail in *Freud and the Critic.*

12. Kenneth Burke, *Counter-Statement,* and *The Philosophy of Literary Form.*

13. Carl E. Seashore, *The Psychology of Music,* pp. 1, 25.

to do with auditory perception, that is, with the perception of sounds, not of music. The great gulf between these isolated perceptions and the sort of perception that involves understanding music is thus left as fixed as ever. Some years after Seashore's work, Géza Révész published a similar study, but with a hint of another kind of approach. Although Révész, too, treats of auditory perception, he asserts that the priority of the *gestalt*, the whole form, applies to music as well as to visual images, provided the music is that of our own culture.[14] He differs further from Seashore's position in recognizing that emotions and physical sound are not related by a simple straight line:

> If feeling were so important, then we should be able to prove its existence and its effective determining force during the creation and enjoyment of every musical work. . . . [Feelings] can indeed set the creative process into operation and occasionally influence the general character of the work, but they are not able to determine its *substance* and its *form*. Emotions are something essentially different from musical configurations. The latter are not emotional experiences but musical functioning wholes (in the Gestalt sense) and their forms are autonomous forms of musical expression.[15]

The term *gestalt* refers to the theory of visual perception developed during the 1920s by Wolfgang Köhler and Kurt Koffka, which stresses the integrity of whole forms, an emphasis originally needed to show the inadequacy of earlier theories that dealt with perception as though it were an atomistic, additive process (as Seashore assumed).[16] Unfortunately, after a brilliant early period of success the gestalt theory faltered, largely because its terms, like "shape," "good form," "pregnance," and so forth, did not lend themselves to scientific

14. Géza Révész, *Introduction to the Psychology of Music,* pp. 93–94.
15. Révész, p. 241.
16. Kurt Koffka, *Principles of Gestalt Psychology*; Wolfgang Köhler, *Gestalt Psychology.*

verification.[17] In the context of the psychology of the serial arts a more serious limitation is the gestalt theorists' almost exclusive attention to space perception. Because almost no study was done of musical or other sequentially presented forms, the particulars of gestalt theory can only be applied to serial perception partially and with caution. Nevertheless, the general insistence on the primacy of whole forms has been richly suggestive, and has influenced not only such psychologically oriented studies of the visual arts as Rudolf Arnheim's *Art and Visual Perception*, but also modern aesthetics, and, finally, the psychology of music.[18]

There are several illuminating recent studies of music based on intelligent speculation that make use of gestalt concepts; these belong perhaps more properly to aesthetics, and will come into the discussion later on. One of the most interesting experimental investigations in the field is that of Robert Francès, who combines a use of whole musical forms with a theoretical orientation linking music with language.[19] Francès compares musical organization to syntax, and shows, through a series of experiments in which subjects listened to specially made recordings of short, complete musical works, that listeners understand the works as forms by recognizing patterns of familiar learned relationships between sounds rather than by discriminating precisely the pitch of individual notes. The application of Francès's conclusions seems to reach farther than to musical structures only, and to be relevant to serial perception in general. Most notable are his observations regarding the detachment that the understanding of music seems to require:

17. R. C. Oldfield, "Experiment in Psychology—A Centenary and an Outlook," in *Readings in Psychology*, ed. John Cohen, pp. 29–47.

18. See Kurt Koffka, "Problems in the Psychology of Art," in *A Bryn Mawr Symposium*, pp. 180–273. In aesthetics see Langer, pp. 105, 121–22, 211, etc.; Joseph Margolis, "Aesthetic Perception," *Journal of Aesthetics and Art Criticism* 19 (1960): 209–13; Carroll C. Pratt, "The Perception of Art," *Journal of Aesthetics and Art Criticism* 23 (1964): 57–62; Carpenter, "Musical Form Regained."

19. Robert Francès, *La Perception de la musique*.

Il y a dans la perception et sans doute aussi dans la lecture musicale, une succession d'actes d'apprehension enchaînés les uns aux autres mais correspondant à la saisie des moments de la structure. Chacun d'eux en nous faisant comprendre—au sens étymologique du terme—ces moments, nous enlève au flux continu. Nous n'y retournons que pour attraper le suivant dans sa relation avec les précédents, avec les enjambements nécessaires aux rapprochements.[20]

At its extreme this detachment from the serial process, in the mind of the composer or the musical analyst, results in "une vision rétrospective instantanée, ou presque"—the contrary of the listener's irreversible successive experience, which stimulates "un travail perceptif original consistant dans la découverte d'une structure dans le déroulement du devenir sonore."[21] At this level of generalization it becomes unclear whether we have crossed over from experimental psychology to aesthetics; a comprehensive theory of serial art meets the psychology of music in that fertile borderland.

Back in the laboratory, there is only one experimental study that I know of dealing directly with serial perception. This was carried out a few years ago by the British psychologist L. S. Hearnshaw.[22] What Hearnshaw did was to print a tape with a series of 2,500 letters of the alphabet, arranged partly at random and partly not so. The tape was then run through an apparatus that exposed only five letters to view at a time. The subjects of the experiment were asked simply to watch

20. Francès, p. 155. It is clear that the *"succession d'actes"* does not mean the succession of single tones.

21. Francès, p. 202. This is a fairly common observation concerning music; I quote Francès in preference to other sources because he has some objective evidence in the background; but the idea is corroborated in Langer, pp. 121–38; Gombrich, "Moment and Movement in Art," p. 300; Donald Francis Tovey, *The Forms of Music*, p. 19; and Catherine Lord, "Aesthetic Unity," *Journal of Philosophy* 67 (1961): 321–27.

22. "Temporal Integration and Behavior," in *Readings in Psychology*, ed. John Cohen, pp. 341–53.

the sequence of letters and make any comments on it that occurred to them. In every case, the subjects first noticed a recurrent group of letters (FFR). As the next step, they would treat the letters in between the FFR groups as intervals, by counting them, and in a number of cases discovering the general principle that the shorter intervals contained letters only from the first half of the alphabet; the larger intervals contained letters only from the second half. Always, the FFR group remained the point of reference. Hearnshaw felt that he had made a preliminary demonstration of the way in which the human mind performs what he called "temporal integration"—our ability to stand off from a temporal series and thus understand patterns that cannot be perceived all at once.

Joseph Frank's notion of "spatial form" in literature, Francès's study of form in music, and Hearnshaw's experiment with serial perception all indicate that temporally integrated perception must have at least two main phases. While we are in the process of reading, or watching a play, or performing or listening to music, the work is indeed presented to us serially; over a period of time. But when we have finished reading (watching, performing, listening) and think about the work, we apprehend it in a different way, no longer as a sequence but as a complete form existing in retrospect all at once. For the first of these modes of apprehension we can adopt Kenneth Burke's term *progressive form,* amplified to include the serial process of any work of literature or of music. Burke defined form in literature as "an arousing and fulfillment of desires. A work has form in so far as one part of it leads a reader to anticipate another part, to be gratified by the sequence." [23] Using the term "meaning" where Burke uses "form," Leonard Meyer, in one of the most influential recent studies of the nature of music, puts the matter this way: "Embodied musical meaning is, in short, a product of expectation. If, on the basis of past experience, a present stimulus leads us to expect a more

23. Burke, *Counter-Statement,* p. 157.

or less definite consequent musical event, then that stimulus has meaning."[24] Although Meyer's theory is difficult to capsulize in a brief reference, its main emphasis, on the organizing of expectation, is clearly in line with Burke's definition.

The role of expectancy in progressive form will be discussed further in chapter 3. Meyer uses this concept in opposition to another way of accounting for our ability to understand the serial process of music as form. This alternative account postulates a combination of memory and anticipation; thus at any given moment we are perceiving the tones being played or the words being read, and at the same time we are remembering what has gone before and forming an expectation of what will come next. But as Francès, who shares this view, puts it:

Ce qui fait la discontinuité de la perception totale, c'est aussi la nécessité des rétrospections: l'établissement des relations linéaires implique toujours la réversibilité—fût-elle instantanée—de l'appréhension. Saisir de rapport du présent avec ce qui est écoulé, c'est perdre le contact avec ce qui suit immédiatement pour établir une connexion imaginaire. Celle-ci brise l'adhérence au présent, qui n'est plus perçu qu' "en marge."[25]

To those aestheticians who think of music as bound up intricately with philosophical notions of time, this idea of loss and discontinuity is unacceptable. Zuckerandl, for instance, rejects it outright;[26] Gombrich (in the article already cited) reports a hypothesis of different kinds of memory, one a short-term storage of percepts, and another more like what we ordinarily refer to as memory. In the virtual absence of any other than subjective evidence, I do not think we can reconcile these

24. Leonard B. Meyer, *Emotion and Meaning in Music,* p. 35.

25. Francès, p. 248; cf. Tovey, p. 183: "Music, being in time and not in space, is never apprehended in a *coup d'oeil,* but always in a momentary present connecting a remembered past with an imperfectly anticipated future."

26. *Sound and Symbol,* pp. 230–35.

different views. It is entirely possible that they reflect a difference in individual experience. I should like, however, even at the risk of adding nothing more than another piece of testimony, to suggest an alternative explanation of how process can become form, one drawing indirectly on Freudian theory by way of a too little known book by the psychoanalyst Lawrence Kubie.[27]

Freud designated three mental areas: one is the unconscious, which contains irretrievably buried material from early childhood, not accessible to recall; the second is the preconscious, the storehouse of ordinary memory, and of all sorts of images and impressions from our waking life. The third area is, of course, conscious awareness itself, which has been compared to the small proportion of an iceberg that appears above the surface of the water. Kubie, in investigating the creative process, makes use of Freud's concept of the *pre*conscious. He notes first that by means of the preconscious we take in far more than we realize. Thus an experimental subject may be asked to go into the next room for a few seconds, then to come back and make a list of the things he saw. He lists perhaps twenty objects. But if the subject is then hypnotized, and again asked to list what he saw, he can list far more, perhaps two hundred objects. Kubie uses this example as an illustration of the wealth of preconscious memory; not all of it is accessible to consciousness at a given time because we select what we shall be aware of on the basis of how much we can attend to, of whether the material meets conscious standards of logical coherence, and of whether it is being affected from below by unconscious anxieties that we cannot afford to let ourselves recognize. The artist and the creative scientist, Kubie argues, are able to make use of the chaotic welter of images and ideas that lie just below awareness. It is a matter of allowing oneself to entertain associations between elements that logical thought would reject as bizarre or irrelevant, and making those elements and

27. Lawrence S. Kubie, *Neurotic Distortion of the Creative Process.*

associations into a new order—a scientific theory or a work of art.[28]

We can, I think, extend this notion of Kubie's to help account for the apprehension of serial form. The work, we might say, is fed through conscious perception into the preconscious, and is thence available to conscious voluntary memory as a complete poetic or musical constellation. By complete I do not mean "in every detail." Conscious perception is notorious for its tendency to fill gaps, smooth out irregularities, and suppress details. This tendency is sometimes deplored, and indeed when it becomes a compulsion it can destroy the richness of experience. But I see no reason why we must have our arts all one way or the other—the wealth of the subliminal *or* the clarity of the rational. Why not both? Only if we have been able to submit to the apparent chaos of a work will we care about its emergent order; and conversely only that order as it emerges has the power to illuminate our renewed experience of the work. The force that keeps any particular work together as one thing rather than a shapeless conglomeration of elements operates in it continuously. Our ability to make and to perceive order, like our ability to use our muscles, is also a need to put the ability into practice. The gestalt theorists inferred this from their demonstrations of the ways of visual perception; and we are responding to the same need when we find that a serially presented work of art takes shape for us even as it goes along.

28. A strikingly similar hypothesis has more recently been offered by Anton Ehrenzweig, *The Hidden Order of Art*. The chief difference from Kubie's position is that Ehrenzweig insists upon the role of the "unconscious," whereas Kubie uses the term "preconscious." Ehrenzweig maintains that the unconscious has an order of its own, incommensurate and incompatible with conscious order. The latter is viciously sterile, destructive of true creativity; it is epitomized in the conscious preference for "good gestalt," which Enrenzweig takes to mean simple regular geometric figures. Both writers point out that a rigid inability to tolerate the seeming chaos (actually fertility) that lies below normal awareness makes it impossible for a person to be creative in science or art or to understand the arts.

If we except certain avant-garde works and deal only with older material, it is possible to make (with Wölfflin) the further general assertion that the aim of art is to create finite works. The quality of being bounded is as essential to music and poetry as it is to painting and sculpture. This sense of boundary is concomitant with (or a prerequisite for) the sense of the totality of a form, its unity. The *whole* form is a primary perception, even in the serial arts; that is, it exists for us without our having to reason our way towards it by joining parts together. This is clear when we are listening to a piece of music; to use a metaphor from Zuckerkandl, the first note opens an imaginative space that is only closed with the final cadence. As a result, what we hear is not just a succession of tones that we somehow busily tie up in an intellectual package, but a whole musical form. The same sort of experience takes place, *mutatis mutandis,* when we read a poem or story or watch a play.

When its presentation is finished (the pianist has landed safely on the last tonic chord, we have reached the word "finis," or the needle has worked in to the middle of the record) we can if we choose look back all at once on the work as a whole. This is the second mode of form apprehension, which Francès and Susanne Langer attribute to both the composer and the analyst. If the first mode yields something that can be called progressive form, the second yields what we may call *retrospective form*—the form we apprehend in memory when the work itself is not actually externally present to us. Since as we saw earlier this detached view seems to belong to our perception of serial form intimately, if not inseparably, the retrospective mode of (originally) serial perception can be thought of in relation to the progressive mode as another aspect of one and the same phenomenon. Experientially, it differs from the progressive aspect in its increased approximation to simultaneity, increased generality, and in being partly stripped of the emotional rhythms that give the progressive mode its vitality. Whether or not we try to articulate it, whether or not it even emerges clearly in our consciousness, the retrospective mode is an interpretation of the progressive, and is used to enhance our rapport with the work.

A peculiarity of the retrospective form, one that results from its generality, is the fringe it bears of half-remembered details —like those other hundred and eighty items that Kubie's reported experimental subject could recall under hypnosis. Much of the twilight fringe of retrospect is available to voluntary recall, on condition that we focus our attention on one part of the configuration. We can thus bring out of the shadows various details which in their turn may or may not seem consistent with the whole form. If they are consistent, the whole retrospect is probably clear and has a quality of depth; if the fringe details do not reinforce the form as a whole, then when we "stand back" again, the details will have to be suppressed in its favor. But even suppressed details are not lost or blotted out; they retain a power to complicate, contradict, or blur part or all of the total form.

In the progressive mode, too, no work of art is as simply linear as Hearnshaw's series of letters. In either poetry or music many things influence us simultaneously: rhythm, timbre, allusion, idiom, and so forth. The sounds of words as well as their meaning, the relation of a work to a recognized genre and of phrases or motifs to familiar contexts other than their immediately present setting, the unfolding relations of polyphonic voices—all these and more have their continuing effect upon serial form as it proceeds, and in our actual experience of a work they are not separable. At any given moment there will be a number of such *confluent factors* at work, some, like meter, helping to maintain controlled forward motion, others, like genre, clothing the ongoing form with its appropriate cultural context.

It is in the nature of hypotheses that we must assume what we try to prove. For the purposes of this study I am assuming that music and poetry, taken together as serial arts, are similar in the things that are indispensable to form (in chapters 2 and 3 I shall try to specify those things), and different in the confluent factors that give each art its own peculiar character. Thus the *tierce de Picardie* and the timbres of instruments are peculiar to music; assonance and the kinship relations between characters are peculiar to literature. The virginalist can use the upper and lower ranges of the keyboard to obtain contrasts and gradations of sound quality and dynamics; the dramatist can hang the heavens with black or call up spirits through a trapdoor. It would be naive to expect precise musical equivalents for such devices, or literary equivalents for the ranges of the keyboard. Artists may use incommensurable ingredients to similar formal ends, and the confluent factors must be given credit for whatever effect they have on the organization of the work in which they occur; but it is that organization, once effected, that may be described in terms applicable to both arts.[29]

29. There are not many well-developed, specific comparisons between poetry and music of any period. Those that I am acquainted with almost invariably use the textbook outline of some conventional form of music (the fugue is the favorite) as a means of analyzing some literary work, e.g. Donald R. Roberts, "The Music of Milton," *Philological Quarterly* 26 (1947): 328–44; Calvin S. Brown, "The Musical Structure of DeQuincey's *Dream-Fugue*," *Music Quarterly* 24 (1924): 341–50; and cf. the incredibly elaborate *Counterpoint and Symbol: An Inquiry into the Rhythm of Milton's Epic Style*, by James Whaler. Horst Petri, *Literatur und musik*, attacks the problem on a broader front, in that he applies a variety of musical models to a variety of modern literary works, but the principle is the same. Albert Wellek, "The Relationship between Music and Poetry," *Journal of Aesthetics and Art Criticism* 21 (1962): 149–56; and Katharine M. Wilson, "The Correlation of Poetry with Music," *British Journal of Psychology* 14 (1923): 206–17, approach the comparison from the other direction, that of program music. Since my view of the two arts is inclusive rather than comparative, it has little in common either with these types of study or with the phonetic approach exemplified by several essays in *Sound and Poetry*, ed. Northrop Frye. The position I am taking is in direct contradiction of Morse Peckham's view in *Man's Rage for Chaos*. Peckham uses an operational analysis of human behavior, and insists that only "primary signs" may be equated between the arts, not formal characteristics. A bibliography of writings that deal with both arts is provided by Mary Gaither, "Literature and the Arts," in *Comparative Literature: Method and Perspective*, pp. 153–70.

Certain types of serial form are more readily adaptable to quasi-spatial visualization than others; and the works of authors and composers vary both in the progressive mode and in the kinds and clarity of retrospective patterns they produce. This individual variation, moreover, takes place in a cultural context of aesthetic habits and preferences; so it seems reasonable to expect that artists in the same culture at roughly the same time will under the influence of these habits and preferences tend to create works having a degree of family resemblance to each other. The same factors would result in characteristic variations of both progressive and retrospective form, and in similar relative emphasis on and interrelations of the two modes. What people experience as satisfactory artistic form changes as culture changes, not in periods that can be boxed off from each other, but at irregular speeds along complex continua. The critic, whose perceptions are in their turn influenced by *his* cultural preferences, makes his historically interpretive groupings partly on the basis of having apprehended the similarities between preferred forms, along with more local characteristics of style, intellectual assumptions and concerns, and so forth.

Like any other kind of criticism, an approach that starts from general observations about the perception of serial forms is descriptive, and must therefore be descriptive of something. It quickly becomes impossible to talk about our experience of art without talking about our experience of particular works of art. After the main lines of approach have been laid out in chapters 2 and 3, the discussion will focus on examples already grouped by history and geography into one nation (England) and one stretch of time (about 1575–1620). In my choices both of approach and of object, I am trying to avoid certain kinds of objections, mainly semantic, that can be brought against the sort of study that begins from a period label and then attempts to define the label; and certain other objections, mainly that of the critic's subjectiveness or special pleading, that might attend a selection of examples from widely different times or places. The more usual approach to theorizing about music is by way of eighteenth- and nineteenth-century works, but the "tonal period" is so easily taken as a universal norm that even the best-intentioned writers are misled by it to some degree. Since we do not hesitate to form opinions about literature whose archaic idiom we must learn, it may be a help towards objectivity to deal also with music whose idiom is just enough removed from that of the later European composers to make us wary of our implicit assumptions. The latter half of this study may then have the advantage of making some things clearer about the music and poetry of the chosen period while it gives a field of application to the general concepts outlined in the first half.

Of the many attempts to define what happened in English poetry toward the end of the sixteenth century, only a few have noticed the contemporary flowering in music. John Hollander's *Untuning of the Sky,* although its evidence is drawn from what poets of the time wrote about music, is not really a cross-artistic comparison, but deals with *musica speculativa,* the learned musical thought connecting tonal proportions with astronomy, ethics, and so forth. By the latter part of the sixteenth century, this system of analogies had become thoroughly divorced from "practical music," the art form itself. What did survive—or was revived—in practice was an adaptation of classical notions concerning the moral effects of music on the hearer; insofar as this is a factor influencing the composition and performance of actual music, it will be mentioned in its proper place later on. Still the best general study taking the two arts together is Bruce Pattison's *Music and Poetry of the English Renaissance;* much the same material is summarized by James E. Phillips in "Poetry and Music in the Seventeenth Century." A more recent discussion, unfortunately very limited in scope, but embodying a fresh and intelligent treatment, is Wilfrid Mellers's essay in the Pelican *Age of Shakespeare,* "Words and Music in Elizabethan England." Since the monumental work of Edmund H. Fellowes in editing and writing about the music of the period, there have been a fair number of articles on particular composers or works, but not until quite recently have there been book-length studies incorporating the results of newer research, and there is not to my knowledge any comprehensive survey devoted to all the current musical genres. John Stevens's *Music and Poetry at the Early Tudor Court* provides a good historical lead-in to the Elizabethan arts; Joseph Kerman's *The Elizabethan Madrigal* is the standard modern study of this important form in relation to its sources; and there are a few other discussions of music for particular media, which will be referred to where they are relevant. Various aspects of Elizabethan and Jacobean music have been presented by Denis Stevens, who had the great advantage of active involvement in the performance and recording of many of the works he writes about.[30] In the same connection Thurston Dart's *Interpretation of Music*, is a lively, if polemical, introduction to the problems involved in recovering the sound of older music for present-day audiences.

The relation between music and poetry has most often been investigated in terms of the relation between words and the music to which they are set—as is not surprising for this great age of song. But even this approach has not been made with consistent thoroughness. Between the time of Fellowes's publications and the present, there seem to have been only a few full-length studies—an inferior one by H. C. Colles on the whole question of *Voice and Verse*, and, by Miles Kastendieck, an unimpressive biography of Campion; Willa McClung Evans's biographies of Henry Lawes and Ben Jonson; and a more recent and ambitious effort by Wilfrid Mellers, unfortunately marred by the uncritical adoption of period labels.[31]

30. For books by Denis Stevens, see bibliography; the discographic section includes a list of selected recorded performances of English music from Tallis to Tomkins.

31. Miles M. Kastendieck, *England's Musical Poet, Thomas Campion*; Willa McClung Evans, *Ben Jonson and Elizabethan Music*, and *Henry Lawes, Musician and Friend of Poets*; Wilfrid Mellers, *Harmonious Meeting: A Study of the Relationship between English Music, Poetry, and Theatre, c. 1600–1900*. Pattison's study is oriented in this direction, too; and see the criticism of Pattison's position by John Stevens, "The Elizabethan Madrigal," *Essays and Studies by Members of the English Association*, n.s. 11 (1958): 17–37.

The best work has seemed usually to come from musicologists who find literary references indispensable. The only attempt I know of by a literary scholar to relate forms in the two arts is Gretchen Finney's *Musical Backgrounds for English Literature.* After a good introductory section on *musica speculativa,* she is concerned chiefly with *Lycidas,* in an attempt to show the influence of particular musical works on Milton's construction of that poem.

Despite the relative poverty of competent simultaneous analyses of Elizabethan poetry and music, one's impression that important changes were taking place in both arts toward the end of the sixteenth century is supported by almost every literary or musical historian who deals with the period; where scholarly differences come is in attempts to define the change with precision. It occurred slidingly rather than sharply, but in all musical and literary genres; more obvious in some than in others, it is never quite absent, even in so conservative an area as church music.[32] Since the transformation, however it may be defined, took place on such a broad front, it certainly seems worthwhile to deal with it so. The great difficulty as I see it is the discovering of terms to describe what one observes, but an approach via the psychology of perceiving whole forms does, I think, offer promise. It appears to be the only theoretical mode besides philosophy that can be sufficiently abstract, and has for the critic the advantage of a dependence on the concrete particular experience of individual works of art.

32. A full listing of even the most important historical and critical works in which the recognition of a decisive change appears is of course impossible; among more recent studies see, e.g., Douglas Bush, *English Literature in the Earlier Seventeenth Century, 1600–1660;* C. S. Lewis, *English Literature in the Sixteenth Century;* Madeleine Doran, *Endeavors of Art;* Patrick Cruttwell, *The Shakespearean Moment and Its Place in the Poetry of the Seventeenth Century;* David M. Bevington, *From "Mankind" to Marlowe;* Gustave Reese, *Music in the Renaissance;* Alec Harman and Anthony Milner, *Late Renaissance and Baroque Music;* Wilfrid Mellers, *Harmonious Meeting;* Peter le Huray, *Music and the Reformation in England, 1549–1660.*

2

Recurrence

Although a work of serial art is (like a painting) first of all a whole form, it can more easily perhaps than a painting be analyzed into the elements that help to determine its total shape. To use for the moment a visual metaphor, a vertical cross section of the form in progress would show what I have called confluent factors, the multiple, simultaneous, and continuous influences upon our response to the work; in the horizontal dimension, however, the serial work is presented bit by bit in a prearranged sequence. This fact ought to make it relatively easy to specify those moments in the sequence, those basic elements of the work that perception seizes upon as guides for its shaping activity. The first problem in trying to understand serial form is then to discover what kinds of elements appear to be the operative ones. If we were concerned with literary form only, the natural first place to look for such elements would be in language, perhaps by way of modern transformational grammar. But that approach will hardly do when the conception of serial form is allowed to include the nonlinguistic structures of music. It might of course be that musical and literary forms have only their temporal extension in common, that their formal principles are wholly dissimilar; but the shared condition of their presentation makes it probable that at some level of abstraction there will be a similarity in principles, too.

Since we do have one piece of evidence relating to serial form per se, which is limited neither to strictly musical nor to strictly literary material, let us begin with it. I refer to Hearnshaw's experiment, described on page 10, with its reappearing group of FFR in a partly random series of letters. The subjects of the experiment apparently did not consider possible symbolic meanings for FFR (like, perhaps, "full frequency range"), did not, that is, think of the letter group primarily as having content. The important characteristics were that FFR was identifiable and repeated. We may refer, then, to FFR as an *element* in the serial pattern. The identifiable elements in a work of art are of course more complex and less clearly delimited. For these we may adapt a concept offered by Francès in discussing polyphony. Francès points out that in a polyphonic work, a sequence of notes need only be continued in a prominent position until the sequence reaches a "point of condensation," that is, until the sequence crystallizes for the hearer into an identifiable pattern.[1] The least quantity of tonal or verbal material required to reach the point of condensation is what I am calling an element of serial form. In poetry, a single word may suffice, or a phrase or an image; in either art metrical units may qualify as elements; in music elements are normally melodic, though they may be more or less affected by the confluences of rhythm and harmonic sequence.

The letter group FFR, being thus identifiable, is therefore an element; probably, since the series of letters was not dependent on learned habits of perception as tunes and words are, it was necessary in order to give the element identity to repeat it. But further, so that FFR would function as part of a pattern, it seems to have been important that FFR was repeated at intervals—Hearnshaw did not confront his subjects with a printed tape of nothing but FFRFFRFFR . . . ; his and our common sense testifies that such a procedure would not have been worthwhile. He might, however, have made the intervals all of the same length—or so we may guess—without destroying the crucial function of the repeated group.

With this last reflection we step beyond what the systematically obtained evidence can support, into a more general way of thinking applied to unsystematized evidence. We have inferred that repetition is or can be a decisive factor in turning

1. Francès, pp. 228–29; cf. L. Meyer on "sound terms" (*Emotion and Meaning in Music,* pp. 45–47).

the temporal stream of our apprehensions into a perception of form. Repetition can happen in three ways: it may be consecutive, or it may occur at regular intervals, or at irregular intervals. Consecutive repetition of elements, in the case of Hearnshaw's very simple material, does not appear to have much promise as a determinant of form; but is this true also in art, where multiple confluences operate even in the simplest elements? There is in this regard the assertion of Calvin S. Brown, one of the few writers to deal seriously with musico-literary analogy, that we tolerate far more repetition in music than in poetry.[2] Imprecise though it is, this statement suggests a fundamental difference in formal principles between the two arts. Let us try to make the notion more precise. "Repetition" ought in the beginning to be defined as closely as possible: I shall restrict it to mean the recurrence of elements that are identical in every respect except for the moment of their occurrence. It is immediately plain that in art of any sophistication, this exception is a vital one. Even the term "element" seems perhaps to isolate something that cannot in fact be separated from the whole of which it is a part, and its recurrence at a different point of time will usually involve a different context, which will influence our understanding of the repeated element itself. Such a thing as "identity" does not, strictly speaking, really exist. Still, I think the term can be used if we agree that by saying two elements are identical, we mean that when they are set side by side without intervening material, any normal observer will pronounce the elements

2. *Music and Literature: A Comparison of the Arts,* pp. 104–11. Brown includes in the term "repetition" not only rhyme and refrain, but also synonymous phrases, metaphors, and internal plot analogues; he considers the repetition of ideas in poetry equivalent to the repetition of thematic material in music. This leads him into serious difficulties when he tries to find poetic equivalents for the musical A B A form (pp. 136–39). The notion that repetition is the rule in music but anathema in poetry is a common one; e.g. "Words can be repeated on rare occasions for some particular purpose, but music thrives on repetition, and the same fragment can be repeated over and over again without losing its meaning" (Imogen Holst, *Tune,* p. 13). I do not think this is true.

to be one and the same. What, then, happens when an element is repeated without intervening material in a work of art?

Consider, for examples, Lear's "Never, never, never, never, never," and (not just an element but) the second section of a madrigal, like Wilbye's *Thus saith my Cloris bright*.[3] The first example as it appears on the printed page is simply the same word five times over; but we may justly question whether those five words as spoken by a good actor would ever be really quite alike. In fact, the whole point of the line depends upon making the words more or less subtly *un*like, by means of tempo and inflection. Were this variation not made, the line would sink into the inanity of Justice Shallow's "Davy, Davy, Davy." Shakespeare gives Lear a series of consecutive repetitions for the purpose of dramatizing extreme stress, and relies on the actor to transform the word as it recurs, to exploit, by supplying relevant confluent variations, its possibilities of communicating feeling. Much the same thing is true, I think, in many other cases where a word or phrase is consecutively repeated: Dryden's "None but the brave . . ."; Frost's "And miles to go before I sleep." Shallow's more limited choice is to exclude confluent variation, and this it seems must inevitably imply a degree of imbecility in the speaker. Beyond these choices and perhaps related to both lies repetition as incantation, where the aim is to deaden thought, casting a spell on speaker and hearer. Consecutive repetition of this kind seems able to transform and expand feeling, and/or to silence discursive reasoning; but it does not seem to function in a larger way, as a determinant of form.

In late sixteenth-century music the literal repetition of motives is not usual, which is why I have been forced to choose an example involving repetition of an entire section. (This fact ought, incidentally, to put us on our guard against statements about music that assume the universality of eighteenth-century European conventions.) The consecutive repetition of part of a piece of music, if we continue to use "repetition" in its nar-

---

3. John Wilbye, *First Set of Madrigals* (1598), pp. 44–47.

row sense, is apt to involve far bigger parts of the work than
mere elements. As in poetry, the reiteration of a tiny phrase
without variation of timbre, tempo, or dynamics would merely
try our patience, as for instance when the record player rides
the same groove over and over and over, or when the boy next
door is practicing a tricky passage on his cornet. So far from
enjoying musical repetition of this literal kind, we are willing
to go to some lengths to avoid it. The consecutive repetition
that we do enjoy differs so greatly in the quantitative dimension that its difference is, I believe, qualitative. Thus, the example I suggest by Wilbye involves not a phrase but a section
about half the length of the entire work; it is in that respect
similar to the repeated development section in eighteenth-
century sonata form, and appears to serve a similar purpose.
It should be noted that in performance, neither Renaissance
nor classical examples would necessarily present an exact repetition: it appears to have been a general rule that for repeats
in a five-part madrigal, the two sopranos exchanged parts; and
in any kind of solo work of either century, the performer was
expected to improvise embellishments the second time around,
as is sometimes true in popular music today. For that reason
I have chosen an example in which the repetition presumably
must be exact (*Thus saith my Cloris bright* is in four parts),
although this is by no means the universal rule.

Once granted that the thing occurs, we must ask what consecutive repetition of this kind does for our perception of the
musical form. The work is, after all, not incomplete without it;
the final cadence is just as clearly there the first time as the
second. Part of the motivation for the repeat is surely the relatively fleeting nature of the musical experience: for many
listeners, this experience is not reinforced by imaginative vis-
ualizations such as accompany the reading of narrative; and
furthermore, there is the question of length—it was a rare
work, in Wilbye's time, that would have taken as much as ten
minutes to perform. It would be an even rarer listener who
could take in every detail of this rapidly moving polyphony
at a single hearing, even if (perhaps even less if) the listener

was "inside" the work, singing a part. That need not mean
every technical detail apparent to the musicologist's scrutiny;
the casual hearer, if he is pleased at all, will probably find
more to be pleased about in the music's second exposure. In
a performance intended to give delight to more than one person, it is no more possible for the performer than it is for the
listener to go back and re-experience this or that moment; one
cannot reread, as it were, the way a reader alone with a book
can do. If there is to be any reperusal on the spot, it has to be
built into the musical work itself. The reader, or the musician
performing all alone, is free to choose what parts to go over
again, but the listener or the musician performing with or for
others has no such freedom. All the better then if he can
expect a second chance at part of the work (the artistic conventions of his era will usually determine which part). Except
insofar as to repeat a given section of a work emphasizes its
relative discreteness as a section, such consecutive repetition
seems to operate more as a reinforcement of the perceived form
of the section than as a decisive factor in the structure of the
work as a whole.[4]

Not only may elements or sections be repeated, but confluent
factors may have a repetitive character, as for example the
rhythm of a dance. I have in mind only the very obviously repetitive rhythms characteristic of music designed to accompany
and guide social dancing, not the more subtle, varied rhythms
to which a professional performer may be expected to respond.
Surely, whether the dance in question is a galliard or today's
latest adolescent craze, nothing can be more insistently repetitive and at the same time more fundamental to the structure
of the music in which they occur than these rhythmic patterns.
It nevertheless appears on closer examination that a piece of
music for dancing is less strictly governed by consecutive exact
repetition than we might at first suppose. Within the period
to which I am loosely limiting the selection of data, I know

4. On kinds and effects of recurrence, cf. Barbara H. Smith, *Poetic Closure,* pp. 38–45 and 75–77.

of no example of dance music in which so much as the melodic line, not to mention other parts, simply reproduces the rhythmic pattern. There are for example no galliards that consist melodically of a single six-beat phrase repeated over and over. This is one of those facts so obvious as to be almost invisible: at every repetition of the rhythmic pattern the whole musical configuration is different because the integral and simultaneously presented melodic line (not to mention other parts, or the steps of the dance itself) is at a different stage. Confluent repetition docs not then have the same value for perception as does repetition of an element. It belongs, as we shall see, to the forward thrust of the work's progressive phase; in the retrospective or total perception the repeated rhythm serves as a background for a form produced by other aspects of the music. Once again, then, I think we must conclude that consecutive repetition does not and probably cannot be a direct determinant of serial form. As long as we define repetition as being exact, the same argument would hold true for strophic songs (the words are different for each stanza, whether the music is altered or not); and, with added complexities that I cannot pretend to unravel, for poetic meter.

All this brings us back to Hearnshaw and the idea of repetition at intervals. It seems that artists, unlike the experimental psychologist, prefer to place repeated elements at regular intervals; to use periodic rather than irregular repetition. The distinguishing marks of this technique are the identity of the repeated element—it must be exactly the same every time it recurs—and the perceived equality of the intervals between its appearances. Even so strait a definition as this may turn out to narrow the choice of examples scarcely enough; but at any rate we can begin with an apparently simple one:

> Aske me more where *Jove* bestowes,
> When *June* is past the fading rose:
> For in your beauties orient deepe,
> These flowers as in their causes, sleepe.

Aske me no more whether doth stray,
The golden Atomes of the day:
For in pure love heaven did prepare,
Those powders to inrich your haire.

Aske me no more whether doth hast,
The Nightingale when May is past:
For in your sweet dividing throat,
She winters and keepes warme her note.

Aske me no more where those starres light,
That downewards fall in dead of night:
For in your eyes they sit and there,
Fixed become as in their sphere.

Aske me no more if East or West,
The Phenix builds her spicy nest:
For unto you at last shee flies,
And in your fragrant bosome dyes.[5]

Those repeated four words, "Aske me no more . . . ," are by
themselves able to mark off the stanzas for us. Even were there
neither rhyme nor regular meter, even if the intervening material did not make sense, were not even language, still that
repetition would make us perceive the series of sounds as a
form. Concurrent with "Aske me no more," however, is another scheme of periodic exact repetition: the paired rhyme-
endings. As soon as we know that the rhymes come in twos, a
verse apart, the first of the pair sets up an expectation of the
second, which the latter's appearance resolves. (The relations
of one pair to another, of the recurrent grammatical structure
of the stanzas, and the stanza pattern itself are not examples
of repetition but of recurrent analogy, to be discussed later in
this chapter.) That the pattern of rhymes is indeed an abstract-
able one and not inseparable from the meanings of words is
evident from our analytic habit of representing the rhymes'

5. Helen C. White et al., eds., *Seventeenth-Century Verse and Prose*,
1:312.

recurrence by arbitrary symbols: aabb, ccdd, eeff, and so on. The poem owes at least part of its charm to its fulfillment of a neat skeletal pattern of repetition. This pattern, rather than Carew's nuances of meaning and his fresh way of using conventional counters like the roses and the nightingale, allows us to stand off from the poem and to perceive it as a symmetrically organized whole. To the strictness of its pattern, too, the poem owes a certain lightness; in a less skillful lyric we would probably feel that a pattern so quickly and easily grasped was not worth more effort towards comprehension than it required. This is, I think, generally true as well of traditional poetic structures high in exact repetition, like the ballade and triolet and villanelle, and for the sestina in which Colin Clout took such pride. If the chief advantage of periodic repetition is that it infallibly yields a sense of form, then perhaps its chief disadvantage is that it does so infallibly.

Nevertheless, when used sparingly, periodic repetition can outline a structure without straitjacketing it. The most common literary case in point is rhyme, with its many possible varieties of arrangement. Even a fairly strict rhyme pattern, with a high rate of repetition, as in the sundry kinds of sonnet, need not make the repetition burdensome if the form leaves room for a sufficient range of variation in its nonrepeated material. A rhyming sound is after all a tiny unit relative to the whole poem, and can more efficiently perhaps than a repeated line or phrase admit a full use of both freedom and restriction.

It seems to be a characteristic of periodic repetition that it deflects attention from the nature of the repeated element itself and focuses attention on the fact that the element is repeated. This was true, as we saw, of the responses of Hearnshaw's experimental subjects, and it appears to hold true in regard to serial art as well. While this focus is obviously valuable in its power to shape a series of elements into a form, it entails a sacrifice of the meaning, or content, of the repeated element that artists are often not content to make. A couple of phonemes that amount together to less than a word can be given up to the demands of a pattern in this way, but an entire phrase, whether poetic or musical, is less likely to be dispensable. Where a larger unit is repeated at equal intervals, it becomes a refrain, a device more typical of popular than of consciously designed poems, and one that tends either to develop internal variations or to become nonsense. The latter of course will work as a formal determinant as well as (perhaps even better than) a unit of meaning. Take for example this old ballad:

> There were three rauens sat on a tree,
> > Downe a downe, hay down, hay downe
> There were three rauens sat on a tree,
> > With a downe
> There were three rauens sat on a tree,
> They were as blacke as they might be.
> > With a downe derrie, derrie, derrie, downe, downe.
>
> The one of them said to his mate,
> 'Where shall we our breakfast take?'
>
> 'Downe in yonder greene field,
> There lies a knight slain vnder his shield.
>
> 'His hounds they lie downe at his feete,
> So well they can their master keepe.
>
> 'His haukes they flie so eagerly,
> There's no fowle dare him come nie.'
>
> Downe there comes a fallow doe,
> As great with yong as she might goe.
>
> She lift vp his bloudy hed,
> And kist his wounds that were so red.
>
> She got him vp vpon her backe,
> And carried him to earthen lake.
>
> She buried him before the prime,
> She was dead herselfe ere euen-song time.

> God send euery gentleman,
> Such haukes, such hounds, and such a leman.[6]

The refrain lines are simply nonsense—singable syllables and no more. Obviously the important thing about them is not what they say, but the fact that they recur invariably and at the same fixed intervals. This example is more complicated than some, in that the refrain is not a single block alternating with stanzas of the ballad, but occurs in three different forms and lengths interpolated in the stanza itself. And the stanza, as the space-saving arrangement emphasizes, really consists of only two different lines, of which the first is repeated three times, followed the third time by a unique occurrence of the second line. So inflexible is the pattern that we could easily represent it symbolically (letting a symbol stand for a line):

$$A_1 \quad X \quad A_1 \quad Y \quad A_1 \quad A_2 \quad Y \quad Z$$

Here it seems we have an instance where frequency of periodic repetition has been carried to the point of self-defeat. The pattern is so clear that reading the poem aloud, though it would indeed convey a sense of form, would also be unbearably tedious. However we may welcome periodic repetition as an aid to perception, we reject it when it becomes too insistent; we reach a saturation point, beyond which the repetition is merely annoying. The dilemma thus posed by the structural value of periodic recurrence and the disadvantage of exact repetition is frequently solved by making some variation in the repeated element—not enough to diminish the immediacy of its recognition, but enough to give some sense of freshness to its recurrence. In the case of our ballad, the fact that the poem is meant to be sung resolves the problem, since the melody does not cleave to the repetitive pattern of the words. It would be perfectly possible for it to do so; the result would be something like the pattern shown in Example 1. This is certainly an im-

6. Bertrand H. Bronson, *The Traditional Tunes of the Child Ballads*, 1:309–10. Bronson's source for this version is Thomas Ravenscroft, *Melismata* (1611).

EXAMPLE 1

provement over the words alone, especially in the refrain; but it still is a little disappointing. We could help matters perhaps by using two ballad stanzas to one of the melody, so that the repeated melodic phrase would be varied by being set to different words; even so, though, the result is less satisfactory than the original tune, with its similar but not identical shapes of phrases (see Ex. 2).[7] The song, taking words and tune together, thus actually only repeats itself for one brief phrase (the one marked n_2); exact repetition otherwise occurs only in the sung refrain of successive stanzas. If we do not artificially separate music and words, the song avoids monotony while preserving a clear periodicity that gives it shape.

But, as we know almost without thinking about it, serial form is not restricted in its determinants to periodic repetition, whether exact or not. Even Hearnshaw's experiment with repeated groups of letters did not use repetition with strict periodicity, and we may surely infer that if letter groups at ir-

7. Bronson, 1:309. See also Bronson's commentary on p. 308. By "shapes of phrases" I mean the rising and/or falling sequence of tones that characterizes each phrase. The pattern of musical analogues indicated here and further explained on p. 35 is only one of those that might be mentioned; an analysis based on implied harmony would yield a different pattern, simultaneous with but not contradicting one based on phrase shapes.

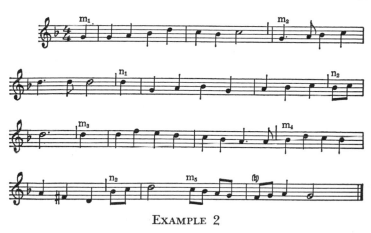

EXAMPLE 2

regular intervals can provide a peg on which to hang serial
form, so too can irregularly repeated musical or poetic units.
The outstanding literary example of this technique from our
period is Spenser's *Epithalamion,* with its unequal strophes
and varying, but only slightly varying, refrain lines. Because
there is so much more at work in this poem than the refrain,
one is tempted to start right off with complicated observations;
but we ought not to overlook the simple fact that the nearly
literal repetition is in effect as much a determinant of the
strophe as the strophe is of the changing meaning and placement of the line.

In fact, though, irregular exact repetition is rare in serial
art. One can surmise that in music it would be meaningful
only to the careful analyst; in poetry it seems to be less useful
than the periodic type. Perhaps the reason that Hearnshaw
used it was due to the simplicity of his material: his FFR if
recurrent at equal intervals would have been too slight a thing
to ask intelligent subjects to remark on. And perhaps the same
half-understood antagonism that we feel toward excessive ob-
viousness is also at work in music, accounting for the very
limited use of exact repetition there. However complex their
interrelations, tonal is at least simpler than linguistic material
in that it does not have a system of reference. Repetition is

after all an unsubtle device, requiring a minimum of attention in order for us to recognize it; it is therefore less interesting than techniques that make greater demands on the perceiver and offer him correspondingly greater delight. Music, as the following pages will point out, is far more apt to use consecutive analogous structures than simple repetitions.

What then becomes of the notion referred to earlier, that we tolerate more repetition in music than in poetry? If there is any truth in the notion at all, the key to it must be the meaning of repetition; the word evidently means something other than the recurrence of elements that if taken out of context would be universally recognized as identical. We have already seen how difficult it is to find instances of such elements. A repeated element can be and often is varied, the only criterion being that it must not be varied so much as to defy recognition. Any part of a serial work, bearing any proportion to the whole, may then reappear in any way whatever, whether varied or exactly repeated; what recurs may be a melodic fragment, a poetic image, a stanza pattern, the latter half of an anthem, a dance tune subjected to variations, a rhyme, a character in a play—any part whatever. All that really seems to matter about recurrence is that we be able to perceive it, that the recurrent part be consistent with itself so that we shall know it when we meet again. A moment's reflection assures one that recurrence so tolerantly defined is a prominent feature of musical structures, and of literary ones as well, and that to reckon up which art is more dependent on it would be mere pedantry.

The ballad quoted above was not, we found, a very precise example of repetition. It would become so when sung right through, because the refrains would necessarily be the same words to the same music in every stanza; but the stanza itself and the use of the tune over and over with different words are better taken as instances of recurrence in a more general way. Within the melody, considered for the moment apart from the words, recurrence is also at work, in a somewhat different manner. The phrases are not completely unlike one another, even though they do not correspond to the repetitions of the words. There are actually only two basic phrase shapes, which we may call m and n (see Ex. 2). The shape m is represented in five variants, which are related successively to each other rather than being all versions of the original m_1. By the time we get to the final phrase, m_5, its relation to m_1 is becoming remote, but it is still recognizably similar to m_4; for that reason all five phrases fit a single recurrent pattern. The shape n_1 is, again, not entirely different from the m-forms; it begins like m_1, then changes direction, and its second version, the tiny fragment n_2, is actually incorporated into the final variant of m. The whole melody is a tissue of closely related phrase shapes, which, whether or not we analyze them, help to make the tune attractive and memorable.

A texture of similar parts is not unique to this example, nor even a peculiar characteristic of folksong; it is a typical feature of a great deal of Western music at every level of sophistication, and can be manipulated endlessly. It serves in the Renaissance to give intelligibility to every kind of theme and variations, to the instrumental fantasia, and to vocal polyphony. In our ballad, the combined patterns of recurrence in words and music are a chief factor in determining the form we perceive. But whereas detailed analysis shows up the patterns as surprisingly complex, our perception of the form is spontaneous and integrated.

This discrepancy appears still greater when we consider that recurrence is itself only one aspect; what holds the ballad together from beginning to end is not only its patterns, but the fact that it tells a story. This particular bit of narrative is not, we may feel, very fully developed—the terse ballad style has other virtues than fullness—but it is certainly not incomprehensible when extracted from the recurrences that surround it. Recurrence, then, must not be a necessary basis of serial form, since if it were, the story could not stand alone, nor for that matter could we understand ordinary speech. Story in literature plays much the same part as familiar melodic and harmonic sequences in music. All of these assist one's apprehension of form by providing what we may call *models*. In literature, by the time we are old enough to call a story a story, we already know how stories operate: the poor but beautiful girl marries the prince, the big bad wolf is destroyed, or to use the currently favored type, the misfit finds his place in society. In more technical terms, literary models are archetypes, and whatever further implications they may have, they provide a means of formal orientation. It seems, too, that not only narrative as we normally conceive of it, but that subtler kind of "story" that governs the progress of lyric poems might reasonably be included in the concept of models. Musical works use models to the same end—formal intelligibility—as poems; that is, music makes sense to us when it is organized in familiar directions round a tonal or modal center. Where either poetry or music abandons its established models, it is apt to rely on patterns of recurrence for its comprehension, if only as a means to establishing new models; where patterns of recurrence are not in evidence, it is likely to be because the work in question relies heavily on some conventional model.[8] Under each genus of formal determinant, recurrence and the use of models, there are many species, but I do not think there are other genera. We shall have to consider the effect of models upon serial form in the next chapter; but first the nature and function of different patterns of recurrence in some actual works of art needs to be examined.

In order to talk not only about repetition, but about the larger phenomenon of recurrence in general, we need terms for the recurrence of nonidentical elements. At this point some help arrives from a previous theoretical statement. George S. Dickinson, writing about music, uses the term "analogy," and defines it as "the association between a given structural unit and a succeeding unit, so formulated as to display similar but

8. Leonard Meyer has made a similar observation regarding what he calls "compositional redundancy" as against "cultural redundancy" (*Music, the Arts, and Ideas,* pp. 117, 276–92).

significantly differentiated characteristics." [9] I would accept
this definition for either kind of serial art, with one small
modification. Dickinson had in mind only those instances in
which we can confidently point out an "original" which may
subsequently be varied; but we shall quickly find that an
original is not always clearly identifiable—already we have
seen that the *m* phrases of *The Three Ravens* appear to be
variations of each other rather than of a hypothetical norm.
When an original is explicit and unmistakable, its analogues
are properly called variations; when no such original is apparent (though it may be said to be implied), its variations will
be explicitly related only to each other as analogues, without
reference to a given norm. In either case, the operative elements are similar but not identical, and different though related.

Dickinson's interesting analysis of musical structure goes on
to subclassify analogy as "simple" or "graduated." The former
is further subclassified according to whether the units are related in "pair, chain, series, or evolving succession"; the latter
according to whether units are organized hierarchically or successively. Dickinson then shows how each kind of analogy may
be used in linear (homophonic) and in polylinear structures,
and mentions briefly "analogies ancillary to structure," such
as rhythm, orientation (tonal, modal), and dynamics. These
seem to me sufficiently different from analogically related elements to merit a separate category. *Analogy* is best reserved
for the similarity between recurrent, structurally decisive elements or larger parts; Dickinson's "analogies ancillary to structure" are in the present scheme included under confluent factors (rhythm and dynamics) and models (tonal or modal orientation).

Although Dickinson apparently had eighteenth- and nineteenth-century music chiefly in mind, it would perhaps be
possible to take over all his categories and find examples to fit
them from earlier music. I hesitate to do this, because even

9. "Analogical Relations in Musical Pattern," *Journal of Aesthetics and
Art Criticism* 17 (1958): 77–84; see also Dickinson's *Pattern of Music.*

though Dickinson's central idea that music is made up of analogues is applicable to many styles, his argument is wholly general and abstract; and it is plain to me that a theory which is intended to deal with specific works of art must be built upon specific examples. Even the makers of the most inclusive generalizations about art base their observations on certain works or groups of works; I do not think the reader should be left to guess what works these are. And there is a further difficulty: what we are here trying to understand is not music alone and not poetry alone, but serial art. There is no way to be sure beforehand that terms applicable to musical structure can be transferred to the analysis of poetic structure, or vice versa. If, as seems to be the case, the recurrence of analogues plays a part similar to repetition in determining serial form, and if periodic repetition is, as we have already seen, a decisive formal determinant, then to deal only with consecutive analogy (as does Dickinson, except for a brief notice of ternary forms and recapitulation) will not be enough. Therefore let us first consider some examples of consecutive analogy, then some examples of what happens when analogous elements are spaced out from each other.

The simplest kind of consecutive analogy in literature seems to be this sort of thing:

> O eyes, no eyes, but fountains fraught with tears;
> O life, no life, but lively form of death;
> O world, no world, but mass of public wrongs,
> Confus'd and fill'd with murder and misdeeds[10]

In this case the analogy between the phrases is outlined by periodic repetitions: *O . . . no . . . but.* The analogic relation, however, includes the series of contrasts in meaning between eyes and fountains of tears, life and merely apparent life, the social world and social disorder—contrasts that are clearly analogous to each other without including literal repe-

10. Thomas Kyd, *The Spanish Tragedy*, act 1, scene 2, lines 1–4.

titions. Taken together, these parallels, like the repetition of
a word or phrase—which we found was actually in most cases
a matter of more or less subtle variation—are a means of communicating feeling. No matter what the inflections of the
imaginary actor's voice, the intended emotional effect is a
crescendo. But in comparison with Lear's reiterated "never,"
there is a sense in Hieronymo's lines of something being built
up; as new words and thus new meanings are set in the same
pattern, the speaker's grief intensifies and grows more inclusive. Present-day taste may find Kyd's device naive, but it is
now as then a staple of oratory.

The impression such parallels give of building up a whole
situation from one point of view can be exploited more coolly,
as in Shakespeare's Sonnet 66:

> Tyr'd with all these for restfull death I cry,
> As to behold desert a begger borne,
> And needie Nothing trimd in iollitie,
> And purest faith vnhappily forsworne,
> And gilded honor shamefully misplast,
> And maiden vertue rudely strumpeted,
> And right perfection wrongfully disgrac'd,
> And strength by limping sway disabled,
> And arte made tung-tide by authoritie,
> And Folly (Doctor-like) controuling skill,
> And simple-Truth miscalde Simplicitie,
> And captiue-good attending Captaine ill.
>   Tyr'd with all these, from these I would be gone,
>   Saue that to dye, I leaue my loue alone.[11]

Since the series is carried further here, Shakespeare makes a
sequence of changes in it, without breaking up the basic pattern of one virtue abused per line—another proof of our constant need for variety. But neither in this nor in the previous
example are these short, closely related elements used to support a whole form. The opening and closing lines of the son-

11. *A New Variorum Edition of Shakespeare,* vol. 1, *The Sonnets.*

net do not follow the analogic pattern, and Hieronymo's lines are only the beginning of a long speech in the course of which they are subsumed in larger structures. Indeed, if the constructive elements of a whole form must be in proportion to its size, these phrases are too little to determine more than a very small work without becoming fussy—as the sonnet I think comes near to doing. A comparable technique in music might be that from Dowland's *Flow my tears* presented in Example 3.[12] Such

EXAMPLE 3

bits of musical rhetoric were the stock-in-trade of the madrigal composers; in four voices it works like the extract from Pilkington's *Palaemon and his Sylvia* in Example 4.[13] As in the literary examples, the musical parallels are designed to inten-

12. John Dowland, *Second Book of Airs, 1601,* p. 7.
13. Francis Pilkington, *Second Set of Madrigals and Pastorals* (1624), p. 58.

EXAMPLE 4

sify feeling, to dramatize the meaning of the words; and although in neither art do they account for a whole work, in
both the use of imitative analogues serves to mark off as a part
the material they govern. The same can be true of prose. Take
a sentence of Lyly's famous rhetoric:

> Here ye may behold, gentlemen,
> how lewdly wit standeth in his own light,
> how he deemeth no penny good silver but his own,

preferring the blossom before the fruit,
the bud before the flower,
the green blade before the ripe ear,
his own wit before all men's wisdoms.[14]

When consecutive analogues are given more scope, they can become more interesting and emotionally significant:

When I haue seene by times fell hand defaced
The rich proud cost of outworne buried age,
When sometime loftie towers I see downe rased,
And brasse eternall slaue to mortall rage.
When I haue seene the hungry Ocean gaine
Aduantage on the Kingdome of the shoare,
And the firme soile win of the watry maine,
Increasing store with losse, and losse with store[15]

The crescendo of feeling is still integral to the pattern, and here the series of analogues not only marks off the part that depends on it, but also relates the part functionally to the rest of the poem. In *Flow my tears* the series is likewise carefully integrated, so that the fourth analogue in the passage quoted is at once answered by a phrase parallel to it, thus establishing its identity as different from the first three.

Subtotal passages of consecutive analogues in music, as Dickinson's article shows, can present a number of different appearances. One of the most common during our period is polyphonic imitation; the quoted scrap of madrigal is typical, but for an instance of longer phrases governing a more substantial part of a work, the passage from a keyboard fantasia in Example 5 will make the process clearer.[16] The first voice entering alone establishes a norm in relation to which the subsequent entries are variations. The second entry, for example, is not an exact repetition of the first; it is a fifth lower, is accompanied in the upper voice, and when we get to the appar-

14. *Euphues: The Anatomy of Wit,* p. 25.
15. Shakespeare, Sonnet 64.
16. *The Fitzwilliam Virginal Book,* vol. 1, p. 19. Hereafter cited as *Fitz,* with volume and page numbers.

EXAMPLE 5

EXAMPLE 5—(*Continued*)

ent end of it, it develops a continuation. A later composer would, besides handling the entries differently, go on from bar 15 to work out a complete analogic structure based on the opening theme; we would call the product a fugue. But Munday does not do this. After bar 15 the "subject" vanishes, never to return. So far the consecutive variations operate in much the same way as "O eyes, no eyes . . ."; but whereas the poetic analogues must rely solely on immediate memory for the impression that something is being built up, the musical example uses this recognition of recurrence and the increasing complication of polyphonic texture to achieve a crescendo both of interest and of sound. Once the theme has been fully presented in four voices, Munday does something that even Kyd with his very formal word patterns could not effectively have done: he at once introduces another norm and treats it, too, in a succession of variations in the different parts; that done,

he introduces a third, and so on. Passages of *Euphues* are some
times like this. Every norm that is adopted and varied provides a focal point for a section of the fantasia, and every section is marked off by a brief cadence. In the madrigal and in
many fantasias the sections overlap, but the constructive principle, imitation, is the same. It was one of the most readily
available ways of putting a piece of music together.

The same preference for varying one strain at a time reigns
in another instrumental form of about 1600, the set of variations on a dance tune. A modest example is the anonymous
Watkins Ale (Ex. 6).[17] Schematically this little piece made up
of three phrases, each of which is once varied immediately after
it appears, would be

$$A_1 \quad A_2 \quad B_1 \quad B_2 \quad C_1 \quad C_2$$

The same structure, but much more extended, was used for
the most solemn dances, the pavans and galliards. In these
the composer often made up his own themes and put forth
his best inventive effort in their variation; the pavan, especially, was a showcase for the performer-composer, not for
dancers.

In songs, as in dances, consecutive analogic pairing is the
rule; it is generally accomplished by letting the same musical
phrase serve for successive lines, or pairs of lines, of the poem.
An example taken at random among many might be Campion's
Breake now my heart,[18] which could be schematized as

$$A_1 \quad A_2 \quad B \quad C_1 \quad C_2.$$

Similar patterns of musical doubling abound:

$A_1 \ A_2 \ B_1 \ B_2$ (Campion, *Follow your saint*)
$A_1 \ A_2 \ B$ (Jones, *Sweet, if you like and love me still*)

17. *Fitz*, 2:236.
18. W. H. Auden et al., eds., *An Elizabethan Song Book*, p. 44. For this
and other brief allusions to songs, it seems best to refer the reader to an
easily accessible anthology; discrepancies between it and the critical editions
are not such as to affect my argument. Hereafter cited as *Anchor*, with page
numbers.

EXAMPLE 6

EXAMPLE 6—(*Continued*)

A B B (Pilkington, *Rest, sweet nymphs*)
$A_1 A_2 B_1 B_2 C_1 C_2$ (Dowland, *If my complaints [Piper's Galliard]*)[19]

Characteristically, once a new strain is taken up, the previous one is left behind, at least till the next stanza; very much as we saw in the fantasia, where the imitative points succeeded one another without return. In either case the analogic pattern has come to govern a whole form.

It does so, however, in a strictly progressive way; that is, we do not find a return to phrase A *after* phrase B or C has been adopted—not until the next discrete stanza of the song begins. In instrumental works, there is likely to be no return at all. Since return, or periodic recurrence, tends to enhance the retrospective form of a work, works made up of a succession of nonrecurring norms deemphasize retrospect, and consequently draw more attention to their progressive sequence. The same emphasis on progression occurs in works that are built up on a single norm—the form we usually think of under the term "theme and variations." The popular dance variations, when they did not vary one strain at a time, sometimes were con-

19. *Anchor*, pp. 24, 180, 215, and 83.

structed in this way; e.g. Bull's *Spanish Pavan*[20] or the anonymous *Barafostus' Dreame* (*Fitz* 1:72) discussed on pages 61–
66. This type of structure seems to be exclusively instrumental. The nearest thing to it in vocal music that I can think of
is Taverner's *Western Wind* mass, of a little before our period,
in which the variants overlap and shift from one voice to
another almost continuously. The keyboard example, in contrast, states the norm in full first, then makes of each variation
a clearly marked-off segment.

To say that variations on a stated norm as the basis for a
whole work do not appear in songs does not mean that consecutive analogues relative to a constant *implied* norm are
uncommon. All of the songs mentioned above are strophic,
which means that each new stanza keeps one of its aspects (the
tune) constant, while the other aspect (the words) is changed.
In effect, then, although we cannot identify any one stanza as
a norm except insofar as music and words generally fit together
more happily in the first stanza than in later ones, every stanza
is analogous to every other; the perceptual effect is one of
consecutive analogues, and is thus generically similar to a set
of keyboard variations.

As long as we do not require an explicitly stated norm, the
same is evidently true of certain poetic forms, for example,
Carew's *Aske me no more*, already quoted. Music for this
poem, by William Lawes, does exist; but since anthologizing
has so thoroughly divorced the poem from its setting, we may
treat the words independently. As I mentioned earlier, the repeated words and rhyme sounds work hand-in-hand with other
patterns of recurrence. One of these is the pattern of meaning: in each stanza something beautiful is lost, then rediscov-
ered in the mistress—the rose and the nightingale after their
season, sunlight when day is over, the fallen stars. The last
stanza, referring not to a natural phenomenon but to a fabu-
lous and symbolic one, departs slightly from the pattern and
thus adds an extra surprise and satisfaction to the ending, an

20. *Musica Brittanica*, vol. 19, pp. 31–34. Volumes in this series hereafter
cited as *MB*, with volume and page numbers.

emotional lift culminating in the well-worn double entendre of "dies." The other recurrent pattern is the stanza itself, with the reiterated difference-within-likeness that characterizes spoken or read poems just as it does strophic songs.[21]

We may add that if the stanzas of a lyric poem provide an inclusive structure of consecutive analogy, so also must stanzas in other sorts of poems, even a monumental one like *The Faerie Queene*; and so also must any recurrent combination of meter and rhyme, down to the briefest couplet. The functional difference between the Spenserian stanza, the couplets of *Hero and Leander,* and the four-line stanzas of *Aske me no more* is the difference in the proportion of the part to the whole, and the presence of other, larger formal determinants. In a long narrative poem the stanza or couplet diminishes in status to a larger aspect of meter, whereas in the lyric it is proportionately big enough to determine whole sections. The latter function is decisive for the retrospective form of the work; the former influences its progressive forming—a distinction that we shall have to take into fuller account later on.

Recurrent analogues need not be consecutive; they may be spaced out in various ways for sundry purposes, as repeated elements can. We found that periodic repetition, especially, tends to dominate a work in which it occurs, and it is only reasonable to suppose that regularly spaced analogues, if they are prominent and memorable, will have similar power. The song forms mentioned above and some dance variations are simple illustrations of this method. Thus if one stanza of a song is organized $A_1 \, A_2 \, B_1 \, B_2$, then three successive stanzas would in effect present this pattern:

$$A_1 \, A_2 \, B_1 \, B_2 \mid A_3 \, A_4 \, B_3 \, B_4 \mid A_5 \, A_6 \, B_5 \, B_6$$

with the vertical bars indicating final or potentially final cadences. But already it seems that analogy is more complicated

21. Smith, *Poetic Closure,* pp. 53 and 108, mentions the use of just such "terminal modification" as gives a sense of closure to Carew's poem. See also pp. 66–67 below.

than repetition, because while the first two phrases are analogous to each other and to all other occurrences of A_n, they are contained within a stanza that is as a whole analogous to all other stanzas. Similar relationships between stanzas and parts of stanzas would hold in the ballad *The Three Ravens*—wherever repetition is not exact in that example, there is the kinship of analogy. Dickinson, though he does not discuss simple forms like these, uses the term "compound analogy" for what appear to be more elaborate instances of the same principle. The defining feature of compound analogy is that it is hierarchic: larger analogues include smaller ones. Thus at the phrase level Campion's *Follow your saint,* for example, shows periodic analogy, but at the stanza level analogy is consecutive; and this relationship will hold true in all such cases. Lacking an institutionalized pattern of recurrent sections such as the later rondo, English Renaissance music offers scarcely any example of periodic analogy that is not consecutive in this way at a higher level. The pattern of alternating analogous units thus produced appears also in the *alternatim* performance of hymns, where different groups of singers or a soloist and a group exchange stanzas; and in certain liturgical forms.

Another way of spacing recurrent analogues, and one that is very efficient in giving a sense of the completeness of a work, is to use the analogue only twice, at the beginning and at the end of the work. The result is a spatialization of the form in retrospect that prompts the critic to speak of archlike structure, or of balance—as though the two analogues were the pans of a laboratory scale. Visualization of forms that begin and end similarly is probably normal, perhaps inevitable (though the specificity of the "mental picture" no doubt varies); so the visual metaphor of balance provides an apt term. Sometimes these *da capo* forms use exact repetition of the recurrent part; but more often the part is altered at least slightly. Wyatt's *My lute awake* shows this method as clearly as one could wish; as in Blake's *The Tyger,* a single changed word serves to avoid the unfearful symmetry of an exact repetition, and to excite interest in what the recurrent stanza says as well as in the bare fact that it recurs. Leonard Meyer calls this device the "principle of return," with the implication that it is universal, but balanced analogues using recurrent thematic material were not exploited in music until after the early seventeenth century.[22] Here and there an example is to be found in an anthem, and in Morley's isolated canzonet, *Miraculous love's wounding*; a related effect was sometimes gained by the use of similar contrapuntal textures in both vocal and instrumental music, but these "returns" are only one among other prominent possibilities.[23] Balancing marks the extreme limits of serial form, and like the stanza pattern of short lyrics, its effect belongs primarily to the retrospective rather than to the progressive form of the work.

Paired analogues may alternate or balance each other but they may also interact in less rigid ways. Corresponding to the alternation of melodies or of textures, double plots in the drama can present roughly analogous sequences or situations, as in *King Lear* or *The Changeling*. Literary criticism is apt to remark upon how these analogues comment on each other (which indeed is a large part of their function), but we need also to recognize that like other kinds of analogous parts, these contribute to our perception of a play as an organized whole, and insofar as they do this, they are formal determinants. Subtotal analogues are likewise effective; for example, the two quarrel scenes in *Richard II*, the emblematic scene in *2 Henry VI* with the son who has killed his father and the father who has killed his son, the opposition of the Palace of Pride and the House of Holiness in the first book of *The Faerie Queene*, and so on.

22. L. Meyer, *Emotion and Meaning in Music*, pp. 151–56; cf. James Mainwaring, " 'Gestalt' Psychology," in *Grove's Dictionary of Music and Musicians*. Mainwaring considers departure and return the *sine qua non* of musical form; after a new theme is introduced to reawaken the listener's interest (in a ternary composition or a rondo), "there can be no satisfaction until the balance is restored and the original theme recapitulated." This seems to me an unwarranted assumption.

23. See Kerman, *The Elizabethan Madrigal*, pp. 132, 159–63; and H. K. Andrews, *The Technique of Byrd's Vocal Polyphony*, pp. 256, 266–71.

The residual category of analogues without a given norm, nonconsecutive, and of irregular recurrence includes despite its negative definition a powerful technique. If most of the observations about recurrence so far made are accurate, it is only to be expected that occasional analogy and repetition will be more evident in poetry than in music; and this does in fact appear to be the case. In literature, occasional recurrence has been the focus of the "new" criticism, and its demonstration is so familiar a critical method that I hardly need to illustrate it here; for a modified example the reader is referred to the discussion in chapter 5 of the recurrence of "light" and "fire" in Spenser's *Fowre Hymnes.* Like other species of recurrence, reappearing words and images bind together the parts in which they appear, and like all types of recurrence at intervals, they can have a decisive effect on retrospective shape. Their fuller discussion, however, must be delayed until we can attend to them in detail in particular works.

Recurrent analogy is then an impotrant means of achieving serial form, as opposed to mere succession. But there are varying degrees of analogy, since it is evident that to sing different words to the same tune provides a much closer similarity of parts than does a tune and a series of elaborate variations on it. The relationship may be as close as twins or as distant as third-cousins-once-removed. Further, the fact of difference may itself be exploited, so that we speak of two elements as contrasting rather than similar. In some later fantasias, a relatively slow middle section may be functionally related by its contrast of mood to flanking sections that are more lively.[24] In small details, it would be hard to say whether the inversion of a scalewise motif was a matter of contrast or of similarity; or in poetry, what relation the various "replies" have to Marlowe's "Passionate Shepherd to his Love"—or as far as that goes, any specific parody to its original. In estimating the de-

24. See Ernst Meyer, *English Chamber Music,* pp. 151–58; Homer Ulrich, *Chamber Music,* pp. 33–37; Murray Lefkowitz, *William Lawes,* pp. 40, 52.

gree of an analogic relationship, as in discerning its formal function, we cannot rely on rational definition alone, because what really counts is how the relationship is or can be perceived once our attention is drawn to it. Perhaps the nearest we can come to indicating the poles of a hypothetical continuum of closeness is to say that a very close analogy is apt to be perceived as identity (imitative entries of a theme, the melody of a strophic song), whereas distant analogy is apt to become consciously perceptible only when we are diligently searching for such a relationship, or in a moment of insight. Most people would, I imagine, agree at once on the similarity of very close analogues; more distant ones are often the discovery of trained critics, and are not necessarily convincing when pointed out—though for most of us, the best criticism seems to be that which makes clear to us relationships we had already recognized without knowing it.

Contrast operates in a different dimension from the closeness-distance continuum. Analogic or complementary contrast is actually a device for enhancing the perception of basic similarity, as in variation sets that use pairs of different techniques in succession, like Gibbons's *The Queenes Command* (*MB*, 20:57). Sheer difference, or irrelevance, seems not to have been very useful to the Renaissance artist, but he may within a context of similarity provided by story or tonality introduce sections with a range of tempos, techniques, and moods, as for instance in the comic underplot of a serious play or in succeeding phrases of a madrigal. The solemn pavan and lively galliard were an early conventional pairing based on similarity of key and difference of everything else. Often such contrasting parts are similar in one way or another; when they are not, they are bound together by the relationships inherent in the model that governs them and by their contiguous presentation.

A final type of analogic relation is that between a given work and whatever conventionally established model it follows. The poet writing a sonnet, say, is making something that is analogous to all the sonnets he has read; and when we read it, it is analogous to all the other sonnets *we* have read. Every sonnet then is analogic in relation to an implied norm, but the norm is different from a stanza pattern such as Spenser's, set up by an individual poet as a determining factor in his own work; rather, the sonnet's implied norm is communal. A sonnet sequence, especially when the same pattern of meter and rhyme is used throughout, as in the *Amoretti* or *Delia,* is at the same time an instance of consecutive analogy and a collection of analogues to a communal implied norm or formal model. Since each sonnet has this relation to the model, independently of other sonnets in the sequence, its relation to its neighbors in the sequence is dispensable. For the same reason, a paired pavan and galliard are related primarily by contiguity, because each member of the pair is simultaneously and more closely related to the implied norm of its own type.

3

Form as Process; Form as Product

The recognition of recurrent elements in a work of art presupposes some measure of aloofness from the temporal stream of events. Patterns of nonconsecutive recurrence especially seem to encourage detachment, since in order to recognize them at all, we must hold more than one passing moment present to our minds at the same time. If the recurrence is obvious and regular, it quickly creates for us an abstract pattern that shapes and contains the work or part of a work in which it occurs. Such a pattern thus counteracts its own seriality, forcing us to step back mentally out of the stream of process and to apprehend the pattern in a single retrospective glance. Where the recurrence is more subtle and is modified by analogic variation and by confluent factors, it may not even be consciously recognized until we are familiar with the work and the pattern of recurrence finally can be perceived under its disguises. Before it is consciously identified, the veiled pattern contributes to our sense of the work's shapeliness, but only when the perception becomes conscious do we know what the shape is.

Detachment goes along with the recognition of pattern. The retrospective form belongs to the furthest point of detachment that retains a significant relation to the work: the point at which we are no longer engaged with the work itself at all, but only with the recollection of it. But as similarity has its continuum, so too has detachment; and the opposite pole from retrospect is the moment-to-moment actual experience of the work. We shall find that the poles are less antithetical than complementary.

The experience of the work in process includes some recognition of patterns as they take shape, but its most striking aspect is our sense of the forward thrust of the form. Leonard Meyer, whose analysis of music deals principally with this forward motion, is right I think to explain it in terms of expectation, to insist that the real power comes not from past moments that urge us on, but from the ambiguous future that draws us. Meyer's theory seems to me the most adequate yet devised concerning the factors that propel serial form. Since my own view of the matter owes a great deal to his, the best way to introduce this part of the discussion will be to offer as concise a summary of Meyer's thought as its comprehensiveness permits. He has modified some of his views in the recent *Music, the Arts, and Ideas,* but his general approach is still much the same as in the earlier *Emotion and Meaning in Music.*[1] There, Meyer begins with the psychological fact that a stimulus awakens a tendency to respond. When for any reason the response is inhibited, the result is affect, or emotion. It is this sort of generalized arousal of feeling that Meyer believes occurs when we listen to music. An incompleted sequence of tones, which we know to be incomplete if we are familiar with the context of musical style to which the sequence belongs, is an ambiguous stimulus. We do not know exactly what will come next, and because of this ambiguity our desire for completeness and clarity is aroused. The musical stimulus indicates "other musical events which are about to happen" (p. 35), and thereby excites the expectation that the tonal pattern will be resolved in one of the ways that our musical experience since infancy has made familiar to us. If the resolution is delayed, or if the structure of the stimulus is not clear, our need to perceive comprehensible forms (a postulate that Meyer borrows from Gestalt psychology) is awakened. We are in suspense, a suspense that Meyer notes "is aesthetically valueless unless it is followed by a release which is understandable in its given context" (p. 28). An appropriate resolution or release of tension constitutes what Meyer, after Koffka, terms "good continuation," further de-

1. Page numbers in my text refer to *Emotion and Meaning in Music.*

fined as "the smooth curve of motion and continuous velocity" (p. 92).[2]

The norm of musical progression is "process continuation" (p. 93), which includes consecutive analogy and repetition, and also the step-by-step progress of the scale or a sequence of equal intervals. This continuation creates tension, because "the point at which the process will be broken or the series concluded is in doubt" (p. 169). It is only at the "point of reversal," when the process is changed and replaced by another mode of continuation, that "the listener finally is able to envisage his goal with any degree of certainty. It is thus the point of reversal of process which constitutes the climax and turning point of the passage, the point at which doubt and anxiety are replaced by more certain anticipation" (p. 171). The example from *"Flow my tears"* on page 40 (Ex. 3) would illustrate reversal very simply: the iterative two-note figure is modified at the words "and weary days," and the resulting four-note figure is at once imitated, thus confirming a new process.

Such climactic sequences are not inevitable; consecutive analogy may also be a basis for "the principle of successive comparison" (p. 152). Variation sets are obvious examples of this alternative process, in which "a given pattern establishes an intra-opus norm, a base for expectation within the particular piece. Subsequent deviations from the pattern, occurring in repetitions, give rise to affective or aesthetic responses because they function to arrest or inhibit the tendency toward precise repetition" (p. 152). A problem arises here, since Meyer elsewhere asserts that repetition is not the basic tendency, and that "one of the absolute and necessary conditions for the apprehension of shape, for the perception of any relationships at all, no matter what the style, is the existence of similarties *and differences* among the several stimuli which constitute the series under consideration" (pp. 157–58; my italics). In the last chapter we had occasion to notice that consecutive exact repetition or close analogy becomes tedious; Meyer's term for this re-

2. Koffka, *Principles of Gestalt Psychology,* pp. 302–03.

sponse is "saturation." The "tendency toward precise repetition" that he mentions seems to have been a tentative proposal, since in the later book Meyer reaffirms the need for variety.[3] The concept of successive comparison is in any case a valuable one, descriptive of the way in which we apprehend consecutive analogy. We do so not only in the forward-leaning attitude that Meyer chiefly insists upon, but with a measure of detachment that permits us to compare what is now happening and may happen next with what has already happened.

All sorts of musical progression, Meyer argues, make deliberate use of ambiguity in order to create the expectation that the ambiguity will be clarified. Our faith in the artist's intention and ability to provide clarification keeps the expectancy within bounds; because we believe that it will all come out right, our interest does not become anxiety. When clarification or resolution does come, the entire series appears intelligible. By his emotional investment in the musical process and by his trust in the composer, the listener is able to participate in the work, to achieve a sense of control over its progression.

Musical organization is hierarchic, Meyer says, since "as the later stages of the musical process establish new relationships with the stimulus, new meanings arise. These later meanings coexist in memory with the earlier ones and combining with them, constitute the meaning of the work as total experience" (p. 37). This highest level of organization (retrospective form) is not, however, the entire meaning, since the lower terms are not only means to it but remain ends in themselves. If we know what conventional form is relevant to a given work, this knowledge creates a special kind of expectation of the probable sequence of events. And since every work we hear modifies our notion of musical norms, we will base our rehearing of a familiar work on slightly changed expectations at each occasion.

I have summarized the core of Meyer's theory at some length because its emphasis on continuous process helps to fill a gap

---

3. L. Meyer, *Music, the Arts, and Ideas*, pp. 50–52.

left in our consideration of recurrence. The concept of guided expectation which is resolved in such a way as to produce intelligible form can be applied, with some modification in its details, to the progress of literary as well as musical works. We ought to be aware from the outset, however, of a hidden pitfall in the way of a theory of expectation, one that it seems almost impossible to avoid. This is the temptation to set up a fiction of virgin experience; that is, to use as a paradigm the supposed first hearing or reading of a work. Most of the musical and literary works that we hear or read announce themselves from the outset as belonging to some familiar genre, to a communal model that we recognize. We do not, therefore, proceed through these works as through completely unknown territory; we know in general what to expect in the way of plot, diction, harmonic progression, recurrence patterns, and outcome. When the work in question is very closely bound to the models current in the artist's culture, the general outline of its retrospective form is so easily predictable as to be present to consciousness even on the first encounter. And if it is true that our experience of a work with which we have never before been confronted proceeds along familiar lines, it is even more clearly true that our expectations are modified when we reread or rehear a work that we already know.[4] In either case we are aware of the familiar lines being filled in. The fiction of virgin experience makes no allowance for this fact, but tacitly assumes that every experience of every work is a completely new event in our consciousness.

The fiction is the more deceptive for not being strictly adhered to. Thus one may speak of expectation as though it were synonymous with Burke's "material suspense," as though the existence of expectation were dependent on our ignorance of what is about to happen, and go on to illustrate the expectation by an analysis of examples which is in fact based on the intimacy that comes only from repeated perusal. Any critical analysis is of course normally made in the hope that it will

4. See above, p. 36, n. 8; and Smith, *Poetic Closure*, pp. 54–56.

earn the consent of readers who have not independently carried
out the same investigation; but there is a difference between
that hope and the attitude that critical perception is only uncritical perception brought into the realm of conscious discourse. What the "common reader" perceives, who submits himself to a work only once, we cannot know, because he is himself
unaware of most of his responses and therefore is unable to tell
us about them. We can only know what the critic perceives, on
the basis of his own report, and what we ourselves perceive
after we have examined both the work and our responses to
find out. By that time, virgin experience and its concomitant
material suspense have been left far behind.

Familiarity is a prerequisite of critical perception; further,
the knowledge that we come to have of a work exists in a simultaneous, not a serial, mode; it is a memory that is summarized
in our minds as retrospective form.[5] What we afterwards have
to say about the progressive form is modified by our knowledge
of the whole work, so that any articulate evaluation of the
former is, whether we admit it or not, to an important degree
dependent on the latter. Reperusal enables the modes of apprehension to interact; indeed, it ensures that they will do so. This
multiple awareness, although it is not the same as the single-
minded immersion in process that the theory of expectation assumes, nevertheless need not be open to the objection that to
attend to past moments necessitates inattention to the present.
On the contrary, the present gains in felt significance when we
know where we are, and the general faith that we have in the
artist's mastery becomes in fact the substance of things hoped
for.

With caution, then, let us see how Meyer's theory can help to
illuminate the progressive phase of poetry as well as of music.
The theory is built on a single idea which can be expressed in
several different ways: ambiguity demands clarification, tension
demands release; ambiguity creates tension, clarification pro-

5. See K. S. Lashley, "The Problem of Serial Order in Behavior," in
Cerebral Mechanisms in Behavior, pp. 112–36.

vides release. The development of the theory consists of defining the four nouns, exploring their relationships, and giving
examples. Thus, process continuation demands reversal, and reversal provides release for the tension created by process continuation. For the most part, Meyer does not develop a range of
subconcepts. The general ideas are illustrated directly by examples, and except for successive comparison, reiteration, and uniform progression, the kinds of process continuation are not cate-
gorized. Although this method provides a necessary unifying
insight into the nature of musical experience, the lack of intermediate terms makes it ill-adapted either to the understanding
of nonmusical form or to the differentiation of styles. Once we
have assented to the basic idea and agreed that not only Meyer's
chosen examples but all the music we hear that makes sense to
us does in fact proceed by setting up, modifying, and fulfilling
patterns of expectation—once we have done this, the theory
leaves us with no place to go. The reason for this difficulty, I
believe, is that like so many theoretical writings on music, Meyer's study lacks historical depth. Despite his interesting use of
anthropological evidence to support the universality of his
thesis, his examples are drawn mainly from eighteenth- and
nineteenth-century music, a limitation that obscures the need
for a discriminating terminology.

Such intermediate concepts as Meyer does provide, however,
are similar to those of consecutive repetition and consecutive
analogy discussed in the preceding chapter. As we saw, both
repetition and imitation cease to be interesting if kept up too
long, and the element must either undergo further and more
decisive variation or be replaced by a new element. In the examples from Kyd, Wilbye, Lyly, Shakespeare, and Dowland
cited in chapter 2, it is fair to say that the continuation of a
certain kind of process creates an expectation that the pattern
will be changed. We lean forward toward the reversal, which
when it comes provides a momentary (in some cases, a final) release of tension. An example more unequivocally in line with
Meyer's approach via instrumental music would be the third
and fourth bars of *Barafostus' Dreame* (*Fitz*, 1:72; see Ex. 7)

EXAMPLE 7

The C-sharp of bar 4 deviates from the uniform progression down the scale, and to reinforce the reversal the running figure in the left hand culminates in a last and slower descending octave. But here the reversal itself leads us to expect a continuation, since the A-major dominant triad is only a temporary resting place; the preceding bars have established the key as D minor, and we cannot accept a cadence on A as final—something further has to happen. After the tenth bar, on the other hand, nothing further really *has* to happen. Familiarity either with this particular piece or with the genre to which it belongs is crucial here to the presence, not to mention the shape, of expectation; nevertheless, external factors like a performer's behavioral cues or the printed appearance of the music can be helpful to the uninitiated, as the vocal inflections of a reader or the number of lines yet to go help us to guess where we are in a poem that is new to us.

Within each section of *Barafostus' Dreame* the forward pull is given its energy by the continuation and reversal of processes over short stretches of time; the section as a whole is kept moving by the expectation of a cadence on D; when the cadence is reached, expectation is weakest. With a few adjustments in the details this description could be accurately applied to any stanza of *Aske me no more*: the indirect question leads our anticipation to bridge the rhyme pairs in hope of an answer, much in the way that the dominant leads us to expect a return to the tonic. Since these are conveniently short examples, let us take advantage of the opportunity to examine the parallel more closely.

> Aske me no more whether doth stray,
> The golden Atomes of the day:
> For in pure love heaven did prepare,
> Those powders to inrich your haire.

The word *whether* (whither), like *where* and *if* in other stanzas, sets up an expectation of the question to follow; then the stress of the rhyme falls on *stray*, so far lacking a subject. In order to drop the other shoe we must add the second line—all of it, not just the first three words that constitute the grammatical subject, since even *golden Atomes* does not tell us enough; besides, we need to reach the rhyme. The musical phrase of bars 1–4 demands completion, too, by shifting to dominant harmony halfway through the first bar, and by reiterating the A of the tonic triad at the end of bar 2, at which point the analogic sequence adds its propulsive force to that of the harmony. In these small passages it is easy to see how what is incomplete in verbal or musical syntax demands completion. In both the poem and the piece a bit of known pattern is introduced, and expectation obediently adopts the shape of the rest of the pattern not yet presented.

This particular process in music is sometimes loosely referred to as "question and answer," but in our examples it is plain that the first half of the answer is more ambiguous than any part of the question. "For in pure love heaven did prepare . . ." leaves open a more puzzling range of possible objects than "whether doth stray . . ." does of subjects. We expect a witty turn of meaning in addition to expecting the syntactic gap to be filled. Similarly the fifth and sixth bars of *Barafostus' Dreame* do not return to D minor, but establish through a dominant-tonic alternation a firm sense of F major. By bar 7, this alternation develops ambiguity by shifting to submediant-supertonic in F major, which turns out to be tonic-subdominant (confirmed by dominant-tonic, the rest of this basic tonal sequence) in D minor, to which we return in bar 8. In both examples, the climactic point is reached about three-quarters of the way through, at the point where the greatest ambiguity of harmony or of meaning begins to be resolved.

The pattern of sequence worked out in the words and in the music is by no means peculiar to these two examples. Like a conventional plot, it is culturally given. There are of course other such culturally given patterns, which we may refer to, like conventional plots, as models. In order to distinguish things of this kind from skeletal models like the sonnet pattern or theme and variations, we may add the adjective "directional" in reference to their ability to arouse expectation, to direct us toward what is yet to happen. Each stanza of *Aske me no more* and each variation of *Barafostus' Dreame* may then be said to proceed according to the same directional model. This particular model has two parts: in the first, the shape of expectation is relatively clear, but the ending is ambiguous; in the second, expectation is less clear at the beginning but the ending is unequivocal. Further examples, somewhat different in details of execution, would be those sonnets in which the sestet "answers" the octave, the stanzas of Donne's *Go and catch*

a falling star, or the melody of Campion's *Jacke and Jone*
(*Anchor*, p. 34). The question-and-answer model can be extended over several sections, as for instance in Donne's *Hymn
to God the Father,* where the first two stanzas explicitly invite
continuation ("Yet I have more"), or Herbert's *Jordan I,* which
asks through its first two stanzas a series of questions; in both
poems the process is resolved in the third stanza.

One last glance at our two well-worn examples reminds us
that in them the directional model applies only to the segment
or stanza, not to the work as a whole. I have suggested that familiarity either with the piece or with the genre, or some kind
of visual cue is needed to tell us that *Barafostus' Dreame* does
not end at bar 10 or 20 or 30. Nor would there be any irre-
sistible indication that *Aske me no more* should continue after
the first, second, third, or fourth stanza, if we did not already
know how the poem ends. (The fact that the last stanza is what
"makes" the poem is another matter). Both works are composed on the principle of consecutive analogy; the analogic
relation between segments is partly attributable to the building
of the separate segments on the same directional model and
partly to the skeletal resemblances: equal length, meter and
rhyme patterns, sequence of melody tones and harmony.[6] The
segments are therefore perceived as equal to each other, but in
both works there is a directional shape that transcends the segmental divisions. Variations in a set are conventionally expected to show interesting differences of character from one to
another, to invite successive comparison by shifting patterns
from treble to bass, by division (several quick notes in place of
a longer note), by varied ornaments, and by alternation of
tempo or of rhythmic distribution within the basic meter. The
anonymous composer of *Barafostus' Dreame* chose to put in

---

6. "Equal length" does not of course mean "consuming equal lengths of
time as measured by a stop-watch." In *Barafostus' Dreame* the segments
are of equal length in that each is based on one recurrence of the norm,
the melodic-harmonic sequence established in the first segment; inequality
would be produced by omitting or adding a phrase, not by variation in
tempo.

last place a variation in double-quick time by way of providing a brilliant finish; further, the slowed tempo of bar 49 implies that the cadence about to come will be rhythmically as well as harmonically final, so that bar 50 makes a satisfactory close to the entire series. This rise of excitement in the terminal segment is similar to the rise of interest already remarked on in Carew's poem (see p. 48). Whether the segments preceding the last form an emotionally ascending series is open to some question, but I think it will be agreed that in both cases the last segment is heightened. This, then, represents another directional model, also to be found in other works. Its basis is usually a series of analogous segments (a pattern of recurrence belonging primarily to the retrospective form); the series may show almost any kind of intersegmental variation consistent with maintaining the analogy, but the last segment will function as a reversal by means of a striking alteration in confluent factors such as tempo, dynamics, texture, allusion, diction. In reference to the special function of the last segment we may call this model *terminal heightening.*

Other musical and poetic examples abound: Donne's *Go and catch a falling star* is very close to those already discussed; in the sonnets of *La Corona,* with their overlapping first and last lines, the analogy between segments is skeletal rather than directional, but one important aspect of the relation between the sonnets is the transcendent model emphasizing the last member of the group. Terminal heightening frequently appears in variations on a single theme, like Farnaby's set on *Woody-Cock (Fitz,* 2:138) and the sets by Byrd and Bull on *Walsingham (Fitz,* 1:267, and 1:1; see also below, chap. 4, n. 25, and chap. 5, n. 1). The last examples make it clear that terminal heightening need not imply a graduated rise from beginning to end of the work. Farnaby and Bull put their variations in an order that sustains our interest and admiration by their skillful use of contrasting techniques, but the series are not graduated towards the heightened ending. On the other hand the variation in confluent factors (which usually includes, in poetry, the semantic factor) that makes for terminal heightening need not

be restricted to the last segment only, especially if there are
many segments. The November dirge in *The Shepheardes Calender* shows a heightening by reorientation in the last four
out of fifteen stanzas, the change in outlook being indicated by
the change in the refrain from "O heauie herse . . . O care-
full verse" to "O happy herse . . . O ioyfull verse."

Works constructed in equal analogous segments do not always and necessarily use terminal heightening. They may, as
I have already hinted, invite the graduated rise in affect which
we call climactic development; and the climactic point does
not have to come in the very last segment, though it will probably be near the end of the work. At the other extreme, segments may be arranged only in reference to adjacent segments,
not to any climax or heightening at all, a kind of organization
that we may (adapting Meyer's term "successive comparison")
identify as *comparative* or *associative progression*. In such a
case there may still be development; that is, one segment may
take up and produce further variation of some element or factor in the segment just being finished; the development will
then be coherent even though it is not climactic. Comparative
progression relies on explicit contrast between adjacent segments, within the context of the segments' explicit likeness to
each other. Associative progression moves along by segments
that are implicitly but not always definably related; the segments may have blurred edges, or may merge into a continuous
development. When progression is comparative, segments are
more decisively marked off and are either analogous to each
other or linked by other techniques.

Although sets of analogous segments may provide a basic
structure even for ambitious musical works, this is not often
the case in long poems, where the semantic factor bears more
of the burden of creating and resolving expectation in proportion to the length of the work. A long poem in stanzas puts far
less emphasis on its stanzaic structure per se than on the progress of its story or discourse. Or again, in either art, segments
may not be strictly analogous. A simple case in point is the conventional form of the pavan, which presents three different

melodic strains, each usually with one variation. A poem in unequal strophes is another example of a segmental form without
intersegmental analogy. Longer narratives, madrigals, some
fantasias, and many liturgical settings tend to proceed by overlapping segments that lead into each other in such a way that
each segment is deliberately left incomplete until the last. If
these segments are not analogous, they are usually linked either
by means of recurrent elements, or by less explicit associations
based on generic resemblance between segments and a common
style.

Finally, works may proceed not by clearly marked segments
at all, but by continuous phases, or even (if the work is not too
long) in a single phase. When the directional model of a work
is that of climactic development along a single line, the subsidiary organization is apt to be one of incomplete successive
phases that merge into the continuously rising curve of expectancy. The progression is teleologically oriented; that is, it is
so ordered as to keep us making and revising predictions of its
outcome. These sundry methods may be combined, as they are
in drama by means of the double or multiple plot: alternation
between scenes involving different groups of characters may
both provide contrast and heighten suspense in two or more
lines of development; generally a single climax will combine
the different processes, more or less comfortably, in a final resolution. *Twelfth Night* is a neat example of this maneuver.

The more discrete the parts of a work are, the more important it becomes to link the parts together in some obvious and
unmistakable way, if the work is to be perceived as a single
form rather than as a collection of self-contained smaller forms
having no necessary connection with each other. This is especially true of works composed of segments in a comparative
progression, where the segment may be almost an end in itself,
with the total work providing a showcase for the parts. To construct discrete segments as close analogues of each other is one
way of linking them, as we have seen. In music, especially,

where analogues do not tend to be widely separated, consecutive analogy is often what gives shape to expectation and thus bridges metric, segmental, or other kinds of division. The distinguishable phases of a musical work, whether analogous to each other or not, may be linked end-to-end by avoiding cadential harmony: this is the usual method of sustaining continuity in the madrigal and other polyphonic genres; a pleasant example in a keyboard work is Farnaby's variation set on *Rosasolis* (*Fitz*, 2:148), where the tune itself supplies a ready-made link by closing on the dominant. Segments of literary works may also be linked consecutively by leaving something unfinished at the end of all except the last, as in the chivalric romance with its overlapping and to-be-continued episodes.

End-to-end linking that uses recurrence rather than incompleteness appears occasionally, as in the "coronas" of sonnets by Gascoigne, Donne, Chapman, and others, where the last line of one sonnet recurs as the first line of the next. Irregularly recurrent elements supply another kind of linking between segments: a key word or image or a musical motif that crops up now and again in the successive segments helps to thread them together and to enhance our sense of their cohesion. This sort of linking depends on backward rather than forward reference. The recurrence of a small element is a fully effective linking device only if at some level of awareness we recognize it when it reappears; such recognition is equivalent to a backward reference to the element's previous appearance. Given its recognition, the irregular recurrence of a motif, as in Wilbye's *Ye that do live in pleasures* (see Ex. 16, p. 139), or of Colin Clout in *The Shepheardes Calender,* can be a subtle and even powerful unifying agent. Usually in poetry it does not carry the main burden of determining form, as do the larger and more regularly reappearing structures, like the stanza patterns and whole lines discussed in chapter 2, but it acts as a support to other devices. A more pervasive method of securing coherence in poetry is to associate otherwise discrete parts by a similarity of attitude and reference, such as holds together the "procreation" group among Shakespeare's sonnets. The musical counterpart here is the kinship between successive themes that are not explicitly related by analogy. In literature this method shades over into narrative, in which causal and chronological connections help to keep up continuous expectation; in music the teleologically oriented sequence of harmonies that is made possible by the diatonic system performs a similar function.

Fuller illustration of the formal possibilities we have been considering will be provided by the analysis of a few works in the following chapters, but it may be helpful at this point to collect the general concepts into a brief summary. Whole forms, then, may be segmental or continuous. Segmental forms may show in varying combinations the following characteristics:

1. The segments may be analogous to each other. Their analogy may be skeletal, involving recurrence of fixed elements in regular patterns, or the analogy may be due to the use of the same directional model for each segment—or both.

2. The segments may be linked end-to-end by leaving one segment incomplete as the next begins, or by using a recurrent element to end one segment and to begin the next.

3. The segments may be linked internally by the recurrence of elements at irregular intervals.

4. The work as a whole may follow a comparative progression, in which segments contrast or invite comparison with each other and with a (stated or implied) norm.

5. The work may follow an associative progression, in which segments show a general kinship with each other rather than explicit analogy.

6. The work may show terminal heightening—increased movement, tension, or interest in the last segment(s).

7. The work may follow a climactic sequence, with a gradual increase in tension from the beginning of the work to a major reversal near the end.

These characteristics are not, logically, all the same kind of thing; some apply to certain aspects of a segmental work and some to others. But the areas of application overlap. Specifically, the first three possibilities concern only local interrelations between segments; the last four apply primarily to the work as a whole. Looking at the possibilities another way, we can see that the first four involve some species of recurrence; the last three have exclusively to do with controlled expectation.

Although the seven characteristics are listed under the heading of segmental forms, most of them can belong to continuous forms also. Naturally, continuous forms lack those characteristics that presuppose neatly separable parts; but usually a serial work of any length does have some points of division, even though these may be blurred and irregularly spaced. Thus differentiated, the phases (as we may call these fluid, soft-edged sections) will not be analogous to each other; nor will they show comparative progression, since comparison is ordinarily based on contrast wedded to analogic similarity. The phases may nonetheless be linked by the presence of recurrent elements, and may progress by associative methods. The continuous form as a whole may be contained by balanced analogues at its beginning and end; it may show terminal heightening or a climactic sequence.

At the level of the whole form, the work of art is perceived in retrospect. Though we can identify a familiar directional model from this viewpoint, the model is not actually operating; it, like analogic patterns, hierarchic structure, and the various sorts of linking, can be apprehended apart from its motion. This is a curious fact; but other than Hearnshaw's experiment and brief references like that of Francès to "une vision instantanée, ou presque," I do not know of any research or criticism that thoroughly investigates the nature of retrospective form.

Its existence is witnessed in countless passing remarks, and for most people it has subjective validity; but because it is subjective, it is difficult to talk about. By "subjective" I do not mean that the retrospective form of a given work will be wholly different for everyone who perceives it; that can scarcely be, since the form is the product of the work of art and is directly dependent on it. Rather, the retrospective form is subjective in that it tends to remain private experience: when we talk about a poem or a piece of music with other people, we take the retrospective form for granted, and we usually fail to recognize how important it is in our understanding of the work, and indeed in our understanding of all serial art. This failure can and does result in serious confusion when we attempt to discuss such abstract matters as poetic unity.

When retrospective form is explicitly described at all, it is usually described in visual metaphors. But the retrospective form of a serial work differs from the genuinely visual form of a painting or a facade in being unrealized: whereas our visual memory of a painting can be fully confirmed by looking at the painting, our memory of a serial work exists after the work has ceased to be presented, or before it begins, or as a frame of orientation both including and detached from the work as it proceeds. Its visualization seems to be adventitious; certainly it varies appreciably from one person to another. For that reason, the terms used to describe the qualities of retrospective form ought not to be tied to any particular visual image, if we can avoid it, since to speak of such images may result in a terminology based on what is personal rather than on what is assuredly common. Some of the words I have been using, like coherence, segment, linking, texture, and so on, would apply to any kind of form perception, whether visual or not; nonetheless, there is a sense of spatiality to the retrospective form that cannot be denied. Perhaps our minds cannot deal with simultaneity in any other way than by metaphoric juxtaposition in space. The retrospective form, we might say, bears a relation to the actually progressing work something like the relation that a road map bears to driving along the highway. What was sequential in the journey becomes simultaneous; and although we remember more of our trip than the map can show, our memory of the trip as a whole is cartographic.

But whereas the road map is arbitrarily bounded by the size and shape of the paper it is printed on, the boundaries of the work of art are never arbitrary. (Even in professedly random or indeterminate modern works, one may ask whether the boundaries are really arbitrary or whether they *represent* arbitrary boundaries). This planned and shaped limitation marks off work from world, gives the work its identity separate from everything that is not it. We may borrow from Teilhard de Chardin the concepts of the "within" and "without" of organisms:[7] the "without" is represented in art by the planned boundary, the "within" by aesthetic unity. Further, the ways in which boundary and unity may be effected are subject to choice, the artist's moment and milieu directing his preference toward some possibilities rather than others, just as his preferences in genre and in subtotal aspects of style are directed. The gradual shifting of the preferences is an important dimension of cultural change.

Boundary is most simply defined in serial art as beginning and ending. Although one might argue that other dimensions, represented by poetic diction, keyboard temperament, and so forth, are "bounded," they are better dealt with as contributory factors, not to be confused with whole art forms. Just what it takes to mark off a work of serial art is a matter for tacit agreement between the artist and his public. There may be preliminaries like the tuning of instruments, prefaces, dedications, preludes, introductions, or prologues. The poet may begin a narrative by describing its setting, by giving a background of previous events, by introducing himself in some particular situation, by presenting characters already engaged in action, and

---

7. Pierre Teilhard de Chardin, *The Phenomenon of Man*, pp. 54–59. In momentarily adopting his terms, I do not imply, as Teilhard does, an equation of "within" with consciousness. But the resemblance between certain aspects of organic and artistic structures has impressed many observers, and justifies the occasional transfer of terms from one to the other.

so on. The musician similarly may start with a single polyphonic line and gradually add others, or bring all voices in
at once on an opening chord; he may offer a preamble, as in the
instrumental introduction to a song, or state his theme immediately. In both arts the opening boundary may be gradual or
abrupt, elaborate or simple, and may adumbrate what is to follow with more or less clarity and excitement.

The way a work ends is determined by the way in which the
artist feels his ending should be relevant to what precedes,
and the kind and degree of excitement he deems appropriate.[8]
Both these criteria are dependent on the directional model
adopted in the work, but most models leave some room for
choice. Thus a climactic model does not decree whether the
ending will summarize, trail off quietly, or give one last little
surprise; there may be next to nothing after the climactic point
has been reached, or there may be a diminuendo, a coda, or
even an epilogue. The climatic model precludes a second climax or a terminal continuation so long as to suggest another
sort of model, but otherwise the choice is the artist's. Similar
observations would apply to other models. The relevance of an
ending also depends on what there is in the work for it to be
relevant to. A work whose total form relies heavily on recurrent
analogy will set up a different standard of relevance from one
that relies mainly on the linking of adjacent parts; where sectional diversity has been the rule the ending will allow a different range of choices than where parts have been homogeneous
and either overlapping or smoothly continuous.

As regards the "without" of a work, its beginning looks backward toward all in its culture that competes with the work for
the reader's or listener's attention. It is from this everyday competition that the work must detach itself in the mind of the perceiver. It has a powerful ally, as Leonard Meyer has pointed

---

8. Smith, *Poetic Closure*, to which I have already referred, deals with
various ways of securing satisfactory endings in lyric poetry. The most important of these are "thematic," i.e. having to do with verbal meanings, an
aspect that I have not stressed as such, but which Smith elucidates thoroughly and capably.

out, in the perceiver's "set," his preparatory attention shaped by his knowledge that what is about to happen is a piece of music or a poem or a play.[9] In beginning his work the artist may rely more or less heavily on this set, and different works will employ different means of working with it. The ending of the work also has its outward face, looking forward to the perceiver's return to his everyday objects of attention. Other things being equal, an abrupt or unexpected ending will draw attention to the fact of return; a gradually diminishing ending will invite attention to linger with the work.

9. L. Meyer, *Emotion and Meaning in Music*, pp. 73–82.

4

Segmental Forms and Associative Progression

One of the main purposes of the theoretical approach outlined in the preceding chapters is to provide a way of talking
about music and poetry that will allow us to describe types of
form as they undergo historical change. No theory, including
this one, is primarily intended to uncover new phenomena; a
theory is first of all an intellectual construct that can help us
to understand phenomena we already have encountered. In
observing what appear to be decisive changes in English music
and poetry around the turn of the seventeenth century, I am
in agreement with a large and illustrious company of literary
critics and musicologists—nothing is easier to come by than
sound testimony to the reality of these changes.[1] What is lacking, it seems to me, is a viewpoint at once inclusive and discriminating, and what I hope to suggest is the direction in
which we might move in order to develop such a viewpoint.
The following analyses are of necessity based on my judgment
of what works are most helpful to talk about; they also reflect
my mistrust of the sort of period study that makes reference to
a great many works but gives careful attention to none. It is
not feasible to treat more than a few works at any length, nor
even to refer to every work that shows the same characteristics
as those discussed. The further examples I mention are to be
supplemented by the reader's own acquaintance with English
Renaissance art, which I hope will provide both validation and
correction for the theoretical viewpoint I am offering.

Byrd's motet *Civitas sancti tui* (see Ex. 8) appeared in print
in 1589, in one of the collections of Byrd's Latin church music

1. See p. 20, n. 32.

entitled *Cantiones Sacrae;* probably the date of composition was several years earlier.[2] Although in the *Cantiones* it is designated as the *secunda pars* of the motet *Ne irascaris,* it is a very easily separable second part, and we can without injustice consider it alone. It belongs to the great polyphonic tradition that was Byrd's immediate legacy from his teacher and later colleague, Thomas Tallis. Byrd, in this respect like Bach and Mozart, seems never to have felt the need for radical innovation. Musicologists commonly refer to him as conservative or even austere on account of his lifelong habit of preferring to develop older musical conventions and his avoiding the extremes of musical fashion around the turn of the century. But too much emphasis on his conservatism should not mislead us into thinking of Byrd as out of touch with the changing musical culture of his own time. In terms of serial form, *Civitas sancti tui* represents much of what was current in late sixteenth-century music, and it is primarily these common characteristics that we shall reexamine.

The opening boundary is drawn according to one of the longest-cherished conventions of polyphonic music: against all other sounds that there may be in the world, the musician sets a single voice. Its presumed context is silence, but not necessarily any preparatory attention on the part of listeners. In sacred music this kind of opening may be a means of blending the work into a liturgical occasion or into a mood of "sadness and pietie." A secular work beginning so may use the device for other purposes, as we shall see later on. Here, Byrd gives the solo alto just enough of the first phrase to establish a recognizable curve of melody; the soprano then enters with an analo-

2. *The Collected Works of William Byrd,* ed. Edmund H. Fellowes, 2:158. Fellowes transposes up a tone and halves the original note values. The collection is one of four that Byrd issued to provide correct texts of works that had been circulating in MSS. *Civitas sancti tui* and *Ne irascaris* are indexed separately in the 1589 edition (p. vi); *Civitas* is performed as an independent work on LLST 7156 (see discography); see also E. H. Fellowes, *William Byrd,* pp. 73–74. Joseph Kerman argues for a date of composition soon after 1575 ("Byrd's Motets: Chronology and Canon," *Journal of the American Musicological Society* 14 [1961]: 359–82).

EXAMPLE 8

EXAMPLE 8—(*Continued*)

gous phrase; and thus gradually the full texture is built up.
As we would expect, each voice enters with an imitation of the
first phrase, but after the first few notes the voice is not bound
to complete the analogy. It may do so, but the beginning of the
phrase, more than its ending, is marked by analogic uniformity.
The second phrase, *facta est deserta,* is set to a new musical
norm; *Sion deserta facta est,* to yet a third, and so on. There
is never a return to a previous norm, and never an unmistakable analogic relation between successive norms. Such formal
likenesses hover on the threshold of being definable; they are
associative rather than comparative. Careful declamation certainly affects the shape of the phrases, but there is no musical
symbolism—the text hardly encourages it—and mild dramatiz-
ation such as the descending phrase of *desolata est* is secondary
to the musical design. Given the principle of imitation, that design is both fluent and flexible. The successive independent
phrases indicate a basically segmental form which is counter-
acted by the practice of overlapping: as one phrase is ending
in some voices, the new phrase begins in others. These com-

monplace techniques lend themselves in the hands of the un-
skilled either to woodenness or to a chaotic laxity; that they
result here in a sense of breathless poise is testimony to Byrd's
genius. As is often true, the best work reveals the value of the
techniques it uses.[3]

In particular, the apparently simple principle of overlapping
is responsible for a quality of aliveness. No matter which line
or lines the ear picks out at a given moment, the phrase that
thus becomes figure against the ground of the other voices is
sure to be overshadowed by another voice before it can reach a
conclusion.[4] The voice that has done the overshadowing then
becomes figure, only to be superseded in its turn just as it approaches a point of relative quiescence. At these near approaches expectation rises—we are sure we know what the last
note of the phrase ought to be—and is paradoxically best satis-
fied when it is rewarded not with a cadence, but with a new
ambiguity. Because its outcome is more uncertain, this new
ambiguity allows expectancy to drop a little, then to rise gently
again as the foreground voice approaches its implied state of
repose. All phases of expectancy will be resolved when one
process is allowed to conclude.

When a new norm is introduced, it is smoothly dovetailed
into this ongoing process. The underlying segmental form becomes explicit at the words, *Sion deserta facta est,* set homophonically twice over. Byrd omits the bass in the first setting,
then in the second omits the soprano, moving the four parts
down an octave, and giving to the top voice (now the alto) a
combination of the soprano and alto phrases from the first
setting. While the two lowest voices hold their final notes, the
soprano reenters, with a new phrase for the word *Ierusalem,*
which gathers to itself all five voices in descending order and

3. See Denis Stevens, *Tudor Church Music,* pp. 41–45; and Peter le
Huray, *Music and the Reformation in England, 1549–1660,* p. 231.
4. See Beekman C. Cannon et al., *The Art of Music,* p. 168; and Francès,
La Perception de la musique, p. 225. As Francès points out, it is a truism
that ground influences figure. Cf. *Grove's Dictionary of Music and Musicians,* s.v. "Gestalt Psychology."

thus reestablishes the polyphonic texture of the opening section. In this way the three clauses of the text are made into three distinct segments of the musical work, set off by textural differences: polyphonic-homophonic-polyphonic. This kind of contrast was one of the ordinary methods available to the sixteenth-century composer for drawing attention to a part of the text and for giving his work variety.[5] The habit of alternation, too, was part of the contemporary musical idiom, as witnessed most simply by the *alternatim* performance of hymns and psalms.[6] Byrd's use of these methods in *Civitas sancti tui* results in what is in retrospect a symmetrical form. We should not too hastily assume, though, that this symmetry is of the same precision as the later ABA or *da capo* type. Only at the most general level, the farthest distance from the work, does any such precision seem to hold. The third section is indeed related to the first, but the relation is one of similar textures (imitative counterpoint) rather than repetition or close analogy. The textural variety and balance are sufficient to give the work a satisfying form by associative means without need for a neatly symmetrical arrangement involving recapitulation of the opening thematic material. This preference for what may seem to us loose structure is one that we shall find operating in other examples. The strength of such structures is in the progressive mode, in their imaginative combination of variety and coherence.

The modern listener, accustomed to tonal and posttonal works may at first be puzzled by the nonteleological quality of this music. Although the system of ecclesiastical modes was no longer strictly adhered to by 1580, it still underlies Byrd's motet and provides points of rest and of finality;[7] it was never designed to include the tense harmonic relations of the fully developed tonal system. Byrd's music requires of us a different perceptual attitude from, say, a Haydn mass—an attitude of

5. See H. K. Andrews, *The Technique of Byrd's Vocal Polyphony,* pp. 87, 258. Both parts of *Ne irascaris* are outlined on p. 259.

6. D. Stevens, *Tudor Church Music,* pp. 40–41.

7. Andrews, p. 32.

receptiveness in which our interest is directed to the constantly changing vocal textures and to the emergence of new phrases out of those already in progress. The motet suggests three characteristics of serial form in the 1580s: continuity depends less on a sequence of unmistakable analogues than on associative relations and the successive incompleteness of elements; retrospective symmetry of form may be very general, affecting only the largest subtotal sections and not extending to details; the process as it evolves is of more immediate concern than the ultimate goal of the process.

Turning to literature, we shall have to content ourselves for the time being with the work of less awe-inspiring artists than William Byrd. Lest the drop be too abrupt for any sort of comfort, we can begin with Sir Philip Sidney. To discuss all of the 1590 *Arcadia* in a few pages is flatly impossible, so I shall concentrate on the opening episode and on Book 2.[8] A literary work intended for private reading usually gets the benefit of the reader's preparatory set: he picks up and opens the book when he wants to read it. But writers of every age and of cultures very different from our own have understood the need for preliminaries. The reader can skip them if he prefers, but often (in Elizabethan works other than plays, almost always) some initial formalities are offered—title page, preface, dedication, commendatory verses—to help us get accustomed to our author before we embark on the substance of his work. These preliminaries have of course other uses, social and practical, but from a formal point of view their main function is to enhance preparatory set. Once a receptive attitude has presumably been established in the reader (for a musical or dramatic performance this task would be done by the social and architectural setting, the prologue of a play, the musicians' getting themselves ready to perform), the work

8. All page references are to *The Prose Works of Sir Philip Sidney*, vol. 1, ed. Albert Feuillerat.

proper begins. The *Arcadia* begins with two shepherds, added by Sidney in the revised version, who direct our attention to the thematic areas of amorous devotion and of friendship. Kenneth Myrick observes that this episode is like an invocation, and that it represents in a "speaking picture" the larger action to come.[9] One cannot fail to notice the similarity to the technique of beginning a play with a conversation between minor characters—isolated, peripheral voices whose resonance is their foreseen participation in the future about to be revealed. Their presence here, introducing the sort of narrative to which the term *counterpoint* is so often loosely applied, is surely no coincidence. That intuitive, offhand musical comparison is, I believe, not without basis, but we can only discover its basis by first treating literature as literature. Keeping in mind the formal characteristics of Byrd's motet (as possibilities, not prescriptions), let us go on to the second book of the *Arcadia*.

Sending a character on a journey is one of the most venerable devices for securing linear continuity in narrative. We need not call every journey a "quest," with all the mythical and mystical implications of that term; it suffices that the hero should go from one place to another not his home. As long as he has not reached home, his position is unstable, and implies that his journey will continue. Adventures and resting places localized along the way cannot be permanent stations and therefore cannot be the scene of the story's conclusion. For Sidney's heroes, even Arcadia is a way station: they are sure not to remain here, at least not unless, their disguises laid by and their wooing crowned by wedlock, they should come to the throne of Arcadia—that is, the storyteller might arrange for Arcadia to be endowed with the characteristics of home. But meanwhile, Arcadia is the heroes' most notable resting place, even seen in retrospect as a goal by Musidorus (p. 161), and Sidney uses it as the provisional end of their recollected

9. Kenneth Myrick, *Sir Philip Sidney as a Literary Craftsman*, pp. 115–17.

adventures. That the narrative present of Book 2 is no more than a provisional goal is abundantly clear from the network of relationships between characters. Each of these relationships (Musidorus and Pamela, Pyrocles and Philoclea, Basilius and Zelmane, Ginecia and Zelmane, and so on) has a destiny that we the readers are waiting to see worked out. The very fact that so much of the book concerns the past of these characters gives a sense of presentness to the Arcadian situation, making it more like a drama than it would be if it were the only line of narrative.[10] The continuity of the main plot is being maintained primarily by means of delays, both within itself and forced by the interpolated stories. Pamela does not yet find it commensurate with her dignity to give Musidorus a clear sign of her favor; Zelmane keeps her two persistent royal lovers at bay, though we know she cannot do this indefinitely; and most potent of all, there is the frustration of the stalemate caused ultimately by Basilius's retirement. All these, however, are more or less static, and Sidney obviously wants continuous *motion*. The most effective way to get that is to put characters in motion, which in the flashbacks is exactly what Sidney does.

Musidorus's need to reveal his princely identity to Pamela prompts the first interpolation, a brief skeletal outline of the events that brought him to Arcadia. This episode is itself, however, being retold by Musidorus to Pyrocles, and Dametas interrupts just as Musidorus is about to tell of his demonstration of horsemanship. That line of more nearly present recollection is brought up to date a little farther on in the night talk of Pamela and Philoclea, so that when day returns we are ready to begin filling in Musidorus's hasty sketch. Like all the interpolations, this leaves the main plot in suspension, while (in this case) Pamela withholds the unequivocal sign of acceptance that Musidorus is seeking. He recounts two completed exploits: the first, involving the paranoid king of Phrygia, is linked to the second by the princes' two servants, whom our heroes are obliged to revenge upon the king of Pon-

10. Cf. Langer, *Feeling and Form*, pp. 307 ff.

tus. Then a link to the next episode, involving the king of Paphlagonia, is provided by no more complicated means than the heroes' journey in search of further adventure:

> But as high honor is not onely gotten and borne by paine, and daunger, but must be nurst by the like, or els vanisheth as soone as it appeares to the world: so the natural hunger thereof (which was in *Pyrocles*) suffered him not to account a resting seate of that, which ever either riseth, or falleth, but still to make one action beget another; whereby his doings might send his praise to the others mouthes to rebound againe true contentment to his spirite. And therefore. . . . [Pp. 205–06]

With the upright Leonatus and the wicked Plexirtus apparently reconciled, Musidorus is about to tell the story of Erona, linked to the preceding episode by another journey, this time in the company of Tydeus and Telenor, who are mysteriously summoned by Plexirtus before the Erona episode begins. But Pamela interrupts, saying she has heard that tale, and we make a fourth visit to the main plot. In fact, every section of past history is interrupted in the midst of this same story, four times in all, and three times at the exact same point—with the narrator's reference to Antiphilus's treason. The tale of Erona and Plangus thus becomes more than an episode; it is a full-scale subplot, never brought to a conclusion, although Basilius does succeed in relating it as far as the Arcadian present. In no case is a section of recollected narrative allowed to end with the end of an episode. Either the episode is broken off or, as with Pyrocles's accounts and Basilius's tale, it is shown to be still awaiting completion in the narrative future. Just as in the motet where the end of one phrase is overshadowed by the next, so here a multilinear continuity is maintained by avoiding cadences and by adroit shifting of the figure–ground relationship between the strands of narrative.

Further, Sidney is using associative methods of linear procedure that his readers can be counted on to understand. It is not necessary, therefore, to reinforce the shape of the work

by patterns of recurrence. Instead, he uses a pattern of alternation between the present of the main plot and the past of
the recollected narratives—or, we might say, a pattern of return, always coming back to the Arcadian situation after an
excursus into past history. The recognizable analogues are general, not minutely worked out, and they tend to come in pairs:
the two shipwrecks; the adventures in Pontus and Phrygia
(which temporarily deceive us into thinking the Paphlagonian
exploit will be equally simple); and the slightly more elaborate
successive victimization of Pamphilus by a group of women
and of Dido by a group of men. Characters come in pairs, too,
with some frequency—Pyrocles and Musidorus, Strephon and
Klaius, Pamela and Philoclea, Tydeus and Telenor, Basilius
and Ginecia (linked less by marriage than by having their
amorous object in common), and even the lion and the bear—
but the members of these pairs are usually linked by social
relationships posited by the fiction, or, to put it in theoretical
terms, by confluent factors peculiar to literature, not by formal
analogy.[11]

Since the 1590 *Arcadia* is a fragment, we cannot be certain
what its final shape would have been. I share Feuillerat's reluctance to fill it out with the latter part of the *Old Arcadia*
or even with the 1593 version (pp. viii–ix), because I find it
hard to believe that after their maturing experiences inside
and outside the siege in Book 3 the heroes and heroines could
plausibly go back to the woods and play at Whitsun pastorals
again. The sisters especially have become too grown up for
that. But if we cannot make any sure statement about a hypothetical revised and finished *Arcadia*, it is possible to draw
some conclusions from its parts. The passion for linear continuity is striking. Besides the handling of the various stories
just discussed, it shows up in the wealth of grammatical and
logical connectives: *whereupon, such . . . that, which, and,
but,* and *because* (all from the last ten lines of p. 243)—to say

11. Cf. Myrick, p. 177.

nothing of the relative clauses, infinitive and participial phrases, and parentheses. These devices are indeed more subtle and more integral than Mopsa's *and so . . . and so . . .* , but their purpose, to keep the line of narrative unbroken, is much the same. Mopsa pastes events end to end, with *and so* for adhesive, and despite the parody, Sidney does not disdain this manner of linking. His greater richness of means, however, makes it possible for him to give the narrative line a dimension of changing quality and to multiply simultaneous events.

Let us take a closer look at the passage I have referred to:

> Whereupon, the King (to give his fault the greater blow) used such meanes, by disguising himselfe, that he found them (her husband being absent) in her house together: which he did, to make him the more feelingly ashamed of it. And that way he tooke, laying threatnings upon her, and upon him reproaches. But the poore young Prince (deceived with that young opinion, that if it be ever lawfull to lie, it is for ones Lover,) employed all his witte to bring his father to a better opinion. And because he might bende him from that (as he counted it) crooked conceit of her, he wrested him, as much as he coulde possiblie, to the other side: not sticking with prodigall protestations to set foorth her chastitie; not denying his own attempts, but thereby the more extolling her vertue. [P. 243–44]

Whereupon refers to the king of Iberia's discovery that his son Plangus is keeping a mistress; in one sentence we are given the occasion of the king's action, his purpose (*to give his fault the greater blow*), a hint of his method and appearance (*disguising himself*), the uncomfortable trio of characters (*he found them . . . in her house together*), and the necessary damning circumstance (*her husband being absent*). The king's behavior to both guilty parties is summed up in balanced phrases; then the initiative shifts (*but . . .*) to Plangus, his state of mind, and his rhetorical strategy. This last Sidney presents in an imitation of persuasive oratory, with a chain of analogous phrases:

not sticking with . . . not denying . . . but thereby the more extolling . . . , all of which things are made simultaneous by the dateless present participles. To illustrate further the verbal methods of maintaining continuity would be cumbersome and unnecessary. Anyone who has read the *Arcadia* with enjoyment knows how hard it is to find a stopping place. The editorial division into numbered chapters was an act of mercy, but it has really nothing to do with Sidney's narrative technique.

To say that this technique is first and foremost employed in achieving a multilinear, qualitatively varied continuity implies that other aspects of progressive form are subordinate to it. In particular, the stress on continuity tends to soften climaxes, since the narrator cannot afford to let his readers invest so much in a single episode as to leave them weary and ready to quit reading after it is over. Although it might be argued that the first shipwreck is subordinate to the princes' adventure in Phrygia because the one must precede the other, the two are not in fact presented as steps in an ascending series. It is true that as Nancy R. Lindheim explains, Pyrocles's recollected adventures put him in situations of greater moral ambiguity than do those recounted by Musidorus;[12] but if there is any climactic arrangement of subplot events it is very subtle indeed. For all the complications and interconnections of the adventures, they retain roughly equal valences toward the reader's feelings. Part of the reason for this is of course that no one adventure is fully rounded off—*any* may develop a continuation at some future point, and we reserve ourselves accordingly. Even Pontus, after its affairs have been settled, demands the heroes' services a second time. The extreme example of this reluctance to let anything be finally over and done with is the reappearance in Book 3 of Argalus and Parthenia. Pathos could have been had by any number of other means, but Sidney chose to revive a couple of forgotten char-

12. "Sidney's *Arcadia,* Book 2: Retrospective Narrative," *Studies in Philology* 64 (1967): 159–86; cf. Walter R. Davis, "Thematic Unity in the *New Arcadia,*" *Studies in Philology* 57 (1960): 123–43.

acters. As Myrick points out, the real difficulty in the 1590 *Arcadia* comes from precisely this effort of continuity: returned characters are often hard to identify.[13] The final achievement of Book 2 is in bringing all the past narratives up to the Arcadian present in preparation for an invasion from the outside world.

Although extensive tracing of sources is not feasible in a study of this kind, a glance at one item in the background of the *Arcadia* may be of interest. I refer to the *Diana* of Jorge de Montemayor, of which an English translation by Bartholemew Yong was published in 1598. The *Diana* begins with two shepherds who are lamenting the coldness and inconstancy of Diana, their pastoral mistress. A shepherdess joins them, relates her story of despised love, and the three wander off together. This trio encounters three nymphs and a young woman in masculine attire (Felismena, whose story was a source for *Two Gentlemen of Verona*); all these join the procession and direct it to the temple of Diana, where hopeless love can be cured. On the way, still another disconsolate lady is collected. Each character is the vehicle of an incompleted story which he or she recounts before joining the pilgrimage; at the temple all of the stories are either completed or given a new turn, and the characters are sent on their separate ways. We follow them one at a time, while each encounters further characters with stories—and so on. As the tale proceeds, it is difficult to envision the fate in store for any of the characters except perhaps Felismena; even more than in the *Arcadia* we are forced to rely on moment-to-moment occurrences rather than on the anticipation of a final resolution. In the *Old Arcadia* Sidney complicated this simple additive scheme by the use of flashback episodes, and by relating the characters and events of one episode to those of another; he also gave it a more definite goal by keeping one group of characters central. The 1590 version retains the *Old Arcadia*'s sense of direction, but with a spec-

13. Myrick, pp. 167–70.

tacular increase of complexities en route. If in the *Diana* associative progression is refined and mature, by the time we reach
the 1590 *Arcadia* it is perhaps becoming overripe.

The equal valences of episodes and the many shifts from
present to past and from past to present (thirteen by my count
—far too many to keep in mind all at once) make for a retrospective form characterized by the general impression of alternation and of superimposed events. It is perhaps not quite
accurate to call Book 2 as a whole multilinear; it is so only
during the recollections. While the narrative deals with what
is going on in Arcadia, its line is single; but during the recollected stories the speakers and situations of Arcadia remain
present, too. The past–present alternation is thus one of texture as well as of time planes. Ultimately the retrospective form
is segmental, although individual readers would probably draw
the boundaries of segments at different places. The convergence
of all the narratives on the present leaves a sharply cut cross
section if we stop at the end of Book 2; when we go on, this
unravels once again into strands, but they are different from
the earlier ones. Now Amphialus and Cecropia are dominant
and the action moves out of Arcadia altogether. Continuity
achieved locally by introducing a new phase before the old
one can be completed; alternation between sections in the
qualitative dimension of the serial line; retrospective shape
that seems clear only from a long way off, and not applicable
to details; and a greater concern for moment-to-moment associative progress than for either the explicit comparison of parts
or their hierarchical arrangement in the service of an eventual
inclusive climax—so far it seems fair to say that these phrases
describe some important features of both our examples.

From Sidney's tense, active storytelling to one of Lyly's tidy
comedies seems a journey into another realm. It is no part of
my purpose to obliterate the individual qualities of literary or
musical works; but I think we are sometimes justified in taking individual differences for granted, if by so doing we can
open out a new vision of what contemporary works have in

common. Just as a writer supplies a book with introductory items, so the playwright finds it desirable to ensure a favorable preparatory set by the use of a prologue; only after we have been thus fairly warned does he open the work. But even then, as in *Campaspe,* there are further preliminaries.[14] Two warriors alert us to the fact that Alexander has just conquered Thebes; but notice how relatively little suspense their conversation arouses concerning the action to come. The emphasis is not, for example, on the apparition that stalks the battlements of Elsinore, nor on the magnificent entertainment at Sicilia just drawing to a close—on the contrary, Clitus and Parmenio invite us to contemplate the ways in which Alexander and his father may be compared in virtue. Like Strephon and Klaius they discuss a theme, not an action. The forward thrust of the scene depends on our anticipation of what Alexander will be like when we see him more than on our desire to see a foreshadowed event happen. The next object of attention is Timoclea (who appears only this once), making a verbal demonstration of her nobility; then follow less striking remarks in the same vein by Campaspe; and at last Alexander addresses the captives. His words do not hint at the complication ahead—they simply confirm what Clitus and Parmenio have already told us. Surely, what matters here is not the end to come, but the verbal and visual interchange as it is being presented from moment to moment.

Lest it be objected that *Campaspe* was Lyly's first play, and that he therefore simply did not know how to arouse intense expectancy, let us turn to *Gallathea,* which in my opinion makes a fair bid to be considered Lyly's best comedy. After the inevitable prologue Tyterus and Gallathea locate the scene under "this fair oak," enjoying the "fresh ayre, which softly breathes from Humber floodes" on "this pleasant greene" (1.1), and Tyterus explains the history of Neptune's anger and Tyterus's hope that her boyish disguise will save Gallathea from being sacrificed to the Agar. Here indeed the forward thrust

14. Parenthetical references within the text are by act and scene in *The Complete Works of John Lyly,* ed. R. Warwick Bond, vol. 2.

is stronger: an entire plot is adumbrated, of which the first complication is already visible before us. The second scene performs a like function for another plot: the nymph's lack of interest spurs Cupid, too, to operate under a disguise. Then Melibeus and Phillida act out their counterpart to the first scene, and finally the three shipwrecked apprentices are introduced, play out the first inning of the choosing-a-craft game with the mariner, and conclude with a song. If we use as a point of comparison one of Jonson's comedies, *Volpone* or *The Alchemist*, it is clear that Lyly's succession of ambiguous situations, although designed to arouse our curiosity, is much more leisurely. The connections between scenes are not made by cross reference—Phillida and Gallathea are presented as parallels and their future convergence is assumed, but the comparison between their first appearances is for the moment more striking. The other groups, nymphs and apprentices, appear simply to exist in separate compartments. Continuity from one scene to the next is achieved primarily by placing one incomplete phase directly after another. The focus on process as such becomes still more evident in the second and third acts, as Gallathea and Phillida trade hints and surmises; Raffe takes up with a succession of masters that has no foreseeable end other than making fun of sundry professional jargons; and Diana and Cupid reach a perfect impasse. Neptune's brief appearance (2.2) serves as a momentary agent of dread, but no one in the play seems to be very worried about him.

Only with the beginning of act 4 do scattered strands begin to be drawn together, and here too the process is gradual, not marked by any series of near escapes or unexpected reversals. The apprentices meet as planned, with nothing gained and nothing decided; the quarrel between Cupid and the nymphs is simply dropped. The peacemaking arrangements of Venus, Diana, and Neptune do form a denouement to the Agar story, but it has not been prepared for by gradually more insistent forecasts. In fact, only the Gallathea–Phillida discovery can strictly speaking be called a climax in the sense of a reversal that the artist has been systematically building up to. For the most part throughout the play we are allowed to focus on the moment-to-moment game of rhetoric without undue distraction in the form of expectancy. Continuity is maintained less by the expectation of an ending than by the avoidance of endings. Thus Neptune keeps assuring us that the deceit will fail, Cupid reiterates his claim to ultimate supremacy, the disguised girls "cannot tel what to think one of another" (3.2), Raffe (and by implication his brothers) is ever ready to be taken in by glowing promises that leave his belly empty.

The use of the acting area, especially in *Campaspe* but in *Gallathea* as well, helps to maintain continuity in the visual dimension by permitting characters to regroup and to move from one scene to the next without pause.[15] This continuity operates together with a system of episodic alternation, probably reinforced by multiple staging wherein the court, Diogenes, and Apelles have their proper areas. In the language, the racy dialogue of pages, Diogenes's scolding, and the dramatized anecdotes of Alexander punctuate the more stately or tenderer conversations of courtiers and lovers, which alternate in their turn. Groups of characters, each group with its own style of discourse, are deployed to create the impression of dancelike symmetry that is so marked in Lyly's plays.[16] In

15. See G. K. Hunter, *John Lyly: The Humanist as Courtier* pp. 8, 107–08. Hunter's remark (p. 295) that Lyly, unlike Jonson, "shows no interest in the *liaison de scènes*; his interest is to set the episodes against one another," is applicable, especially to *Gallathea*, but needs qualification with reference to developments in segmental forms after Lyly.

16. Hunter, pp. 97–103, 195–204. See especially the following comments on *Gallathea*: "Almost all the plot material is made out of one motif—the attempt to deceive destiny by means of disguise. . . . One can see the play being built up by methods almost exactly analogous to those of fugue in music" (p. 198). "Where all the characters are arranged to imitate one another, and where the focus of interest is on the repetition and modification and rearrangement of a basic pattern of persons, we do not ask how the persons will develop individually, but how the situation can be further manipulated" (p. 199). *Gallathea* lacks a royal figure as a focal point; instead, "the cast is grouped in such a way that there is a state of permanent unbalance, keeping the action in movement; balance can be restored only

Gallathea the continuity is somewhat less obvious, the systematic alternation somewhat more so. On closer examination, however, the systems do not extend to analogous details or even to contrasting significances. We do not, that is, have in these early comedies an ingenious piece of geometric oppositions as in the later *Mother Bombie,* with its precisely balanced pairs of mismatched lovers, nor a thematic set of contrasts like those between the milieus of the king, Falstaff, and Hotspur in *1 Henry IV.* What we do have is a general retrospective impression of alternation that does not need to be rigidly worked out or profound. The symmetry belongs in the first place to the progressive mode, and in that mode it is confirmed by the final arrangement of the characters in a dance.

Until recently, literary critics tended to assume that English drama before about 1595 was "primitive," that is, the plays of Marlowe, Lyly, Kyd, and many anonymous works were groping attempts at the dramatic (or "structural") unity which Shakespeare and Jonson succeeded in bringing to light.[17] Underlying this assumption is the further assumption that we of the mid-twentieth century all understand and agree upon what "unity" is, so that the term, admitting of only one definition and that universally known, does not need to be defined. But if we are willing to give older works the benefit of the doubt for awhile, we begin to suspect that this undefined modern criterion for unity is not unquestionable. Different techniques, emphases, and artistic assumptions can produce works that show other patterns of unity than the climactic one we are most apt to admire, and other means of progression than the teleological. The works we have just been considering appear to be exploiting some of the possibilities we often neglect, as do any number of plays and poems of about the same time. The episodic

---

at the end by some *fiat* from outside" (p. 204). See also M. C. Bradbrook, *The Growth and Structure of Elizabethan Comedy,* p. 62.

17. E.g. Doran, *Endeavors of Art,* which offers this opinion very narrowly; more sophisticated versions appear in Alfred Harbage, *Shakespeare and the Rival Traditions,* pp. 65–71; and Wolfgang Clemen, *English Tragedy before Shakespeare,* pp. 164–86.

structure of *Tamburlaine* (both parts) has often been re-marked, and variously defended and deplored; so too with the earlier history plays, ranging in quality from crude examples like *Jack Straw* and *The Famous Victories* to more sophisti-cated ones like the anonymous *King John, Woodstock,* and *King Leir.* Verse narrative shows the same characteristic amalgam of segmental and continuous organization as we found in the *Arcadia*—a couple of instances are *Scilla's Meta-morphosis* by Thomas Lodge and Thomas Heywood's *Oenone and Paris.* The sudden vogue of sonnet sequences in the ear-lier 1590s seems to reflect similar formal habits and prefer-ences, which may also have influenced that puzzling collection of archaisms and innovations, *The Shepheardes Calender.*

Drama tends by and large to be more frankly segmental than narrative because of the conditions of its presentation; for re-lated reasons, the episodic quality is less disguised in other forms of music than we found it to be in the motet. In 1591 the scribe John Baldwin finished writing out for one Lady Nevell, otherwise almost unknown, a collection of Byrd's key-board works.[18] It was not yet generally feasible to print key-board music—the first printed collection was produced in about 1612—consequently, nearly all our sources for this music are manuscripts, often undated and containing works by two or three generations of composers. The *Mulliner Book,* prob-ably finished about 1570, is of this kind, and so is the largest and best-known source, the *Fitzwilliam Virginal Book.* Such conditions make precise chronology impossible; the best that can be done in many cases is to establish a *terminus ad quem.*[19] Luckily the Nevell book does bear a definite date, so that we know at least that the works it contains must have been written by 1591. Among them are examples of all the most frequently used conventional forms of the ensuing decades, with a domi-nant emphasis on two kinds of variation sets. Both for their

18. *My Ladye Nevells Booke,* p. xv.
19. Charles van den Borren, *The Sources of Keyboard Music in England,* pp. 31–51; and Denis Stevens, *The Mulliner Book: A Commentary,* p. 18.

intrinsic interest and as bases for comparison with later works, these sets are worth examining in some detail.

The most serious obstacle in the way of our understanding Elizabethan variation sets is our assurance that we know what a variation set is. If we had to explain our notion of how a theme and variations proceeds, most of us would probably come up with something like the following: The theme is first stated in full with simple harmonization; each variation applies to the whole theme some characteristic figure or technique—a triplet rhythm, continuous rapid passages, placement of the theme in the bass, or what have you. The set may end either with a particularly brilliant variation, or with a grandly homophonic one, or with a return to something close to the simple opening statement. This description is not the exclusive property of the musically naive: even the distinguished scholar-performer Thurston Dart went so far as to supply an unauthorized restatement of the tune of Byrd's *First French Coranto;* Margaret Glyn seems to have made much the same assumption; and it persists in comments on the Elizabethan variation form.[20] But it is not entirely accurate. The discussion of Elizabethans by Robert V. Nelson in his *Technique of Variation*[21] is more discriminating, and confirms the impressions of form that result if we put away our preconceptions as far as we can and regard Byrd's variation sets as though this were a kind of music we had never heard before. Certain patterns then appear that do not follow the above description; patterns, it turns out, that belong more exclusively to the late sixteenth century.

As van den Borren recognized, dances have to be dealt with separately from variations on song tunes, even though a

20. Thurston Dart, OL 50076 (I am not objecting to the performer's just license, but it is interesting to observe the license being used in this particular way); Margaret H. Glyn, *About Elizabethan Virginal Music and Its Composers,* p. 29. The most widely disseminated commentaries are the notes that accompany recordings; these vary enormously in accuracy, and it does not seem worthwhile to sort them out here.

21. Pp. 29–41, a good general discussion with illustrations; see also n. 28 below.

dance set may use a familiar melody as a norm.[22] The difference between the two kinds of sets is a rule of thumb: song variations keep the theme whole; dance variations break it up into two or more strains. In the genre of song variations, and compared with later sources, the Nevell book appears to show a mild preference for those that stress the composer's invention, and to omit those on the more arresting melodies. The latter, like *Callino Casturame, Fortune my foe, O mistress mine* (almost certainly a later composition), and *Wolsey's wild,* have a noticeable kinship in their deference to the melody.[23] Of the Nevell group, only *Lord Willoughby's welcome home* (or *Rowland, Fitz,* 2:190) shows this tunefulness, and it is by far the most modest thing of its kind in the book, going through only three variations, whereas most of the others reach at least eight or nine, and *Walsingham* (a short tune, to be sure) attains to twenty-two. In general, the more serious, or composerly, sets seem to require a minimum of six variations, preferably more. Byrd is still regarded as an important pioneer in this genre; it is obviously one that he took an interest in.

In song variations Byrd, like all Elizabethan composers, begins with the first variation, not with a normative statement of the theme to be varied afterwards. The opening boundary may be set either with a chord, supplying this first variation with its tonal frame of reference, or it may begin like the motet, with a few notes in a single voice, announcing the tune. Since the tune is sure to be familiar, it is not necessary to present it baldly, to tell the listeners what they already know. The gestalt of the norm is often implied with the least recognizable fragment, so that its transformation can begin. This method of getting under way operates psychologically much like the poet's device of asking, "Shall I compare thee to a summer's day?" or of presenting a familiar fictional event to be elabo-

22. Van den Borren, pp. 250 ff.

23. See Byrd, *Works,* vol. 20, which contains all the song variations; also *Fitz,* 2:186; 1:254, 258; 2:184. *Works* gives the better text, but *Fitz* has been reprinted by Dover, and is more accessible; accordingly, both sources are given. I have modernized the spelling of titles.

rated: "A Gentle Knight was pricking on the plaine. . . ."
The implication of beginning with some familiar kind of material or of rhetoric is that what the artist is going to do with
the material will be a novelty composed with reference to
works or techniques we already know. I think it is fair to say
that Byrd does not as a rule try to surprise us. As we shall see
when we focus on one particular set, variations do not necessarily succeed one another by dramatic contrasts. The generalization that variations tend to increase in brilliance (or
busyness) until the last, which returns to a broad statement of
the theme, is partly true, insofar as succeeding variations often
use quicker notes and the final variation slower ones. But the
last variation, though it may recall the first, has a more complex function than that. It tends to be much richer than the
first in polyphonic interest, and to rely less than do the intermediate variations on shifts in rhythm and rapid passages. Its
multiple voices thus fulfill the melody in the most venerable
terms, those of vocal polyphony. The full-circle effect is sometimes present, but it is more like the new social harmony established in the last act of a Shakespearean comedy than it is
like the last third of a *da capo* aria, or even the recapitulation
in classical sonata form. Where it occurs at all, symmetry is
like the symmetry of *Civitas sancti tui*—a thing to be suggested, not insisted upon.

Similarly, Byrd rarely if ever makes a variation by taking a
single device and imposing it relentlessly throughout one complete analogue of the theme. His method is more flexible. In
the shorter sets there is a model that governs the entire set, and
the separate variations proceed in such a way as to give shape
and impetus to the whole, or to reproduce the model or some
part of it in miniature. Even the standard device of alternating
passages between the two hands is not pursued with a concern for visual, schematic consistency. The progress of the
variations is an improviser's associative progress, guided by
but not at the mercy of a preconceived goal. The closing
boundary is of course dependent on the rest of the final variation. It is true that this is usually polyphonic in texture and

less given to rapid scales and so forth than its predecessors; but the very last couple of bars frequently do present a fast ascending or descending passage. The theme may even be extended for a bar or two to give time for a little coda. I am not sure whether a brilliant finish or a broad rallentando was intended—either would provide a moment of terminal heightening in this nonclimactic form. The concluding breves that are placed at the end of many pieces in the *Fitzwilliam Virginal Book* may indicate a conventional rolled chord, as a means of setting a period to the music.[24]

All these general remarks are naturally more or less applicable from one variation set to the next; as a concrete example let us take the most ambitious of the sets in the Nevell book, the variations on *Walsingham* (Ex. 9).[25] Probably some of these would be cut in an actual performance, but it is possible that the set is conceived as a whole form. Cuts might or might not decisively affect this form, depending on how they were made; in any case, lacking evidence on the point, we are safest to take the Nevell text as it stands.

By alternating the tune between an upper and a lower part in the opening variation, Byrd brings even this initial statement into the two systems that govern his variation techniques generally: alternation and imitation. As in several of the more

24. See Robert Donington (who quotes Girolamo Frescobaldi, *Toccatas* [Rome, 1614], preface, p. 5): "The closes, though notated as rapid, need to be played in a very broad manner; and the nearer you come to the conclusion of the passage or close, the more you should hold back the time" (*The Performance of Early Music*, p. 367). "The words 'drag' for rallentando and 'away' for *a tempo* appear in early seventeenth-century English MSS., and printed by Thomas Mace (*Musick's Monument*, London, 1676)" (Donington, p. 368). See also p. 508, and cf. Howard Ferguson, "Repeats and Final Bars in the Fitzwilliam Virginal Booke," *Music and Letters* 43 (1962): 345–50. Ferguson believes the breves are merely visual ornaments. Different practical ways of dealing with endings may be compared by reference to the following recordings: HCR-ST-7015; OL 50076; BC 1298; and TV 34200.

25. Byrd, *Works*, 20:24. Unfortunately this edition contains a misprint, resulting in the omission of an entire line. Other modern editions are Hilda Andrews's of the Nevell book (I quote from this, p. 173), and *Fitz*, 1:267.

EXAMPLE 9

extended sets, the musical fabric is built up gradually. If you
are going to have a long series of variations there is no need
to plunge immediately into pyrotechnics and striking contrasts.
Byrd plays with the tune polyphonically, shifting it from one
voice to another with changing counterpoint, and beginning
only in the fourth variation to speed up by introducing an
imitative point in quavers. In general, the first seven variations
may be said to conform to the polyphonic type defined by van
den Borren.[26] Eight, nine, and half of ten alternate continuous
passages between the hands; then there is a reversion to part
writing for the second half of the tenth through the eleventh.

26. Van den Borren, pp. 211–22; see especially the remarks on *Walsingham*, pp. 214–15. The four categories van den Borren offers prove to be
unstable even in his own discussion, so I have refrained from trying to use
them. He places the entire *Walsingham* set in the polyphonic class, but not
all the variations will fit there comfortably.

Variation twelve is like a summary of eight and nine, but thirteen returns once more to the polyphonic texture. With the fourteenth variation Byrd at last seems to shift from composerly to performer-oriented techniques: there follow running thirds, semiquavers, and (in variation sixteen) a favorite bit of virtuosity, the three-against-two rhythmic interplay. This concession to the musical surface is withdrawn as the seventeenth variation ends, and for the rest of the set we return to three- and four-part counterpoint—the kind of work that draws attention to the inside of the composer's design, so to speak, rather than to his ingenuity and virtuosity in producing effects. This last group, however, even though it is perhaps less brilliant than the preceding group, nevertheless gives an impression of intensified movement through the rhythmic interlocking of parts. This is not, to be sure, a "virginalistic" technique, but neither is it a broad restatement of the theme. Byrd evidently felt that such complex sound was unsuitable to close the set, so the twenty-second variation, after its stately beginning, does not move to an equally stately end. A downward-flowing scale interrupts the cadence, and thrusts forward like an anacrusis to the flying runs of the coda (see Ex. 10).

Whatever selections a performer might make for practical reasons, the real business of the set as we have it is an exploration of keyboard polyphonic design.[27] It is thus more like a fantasy on a single subject than it is like a collection of settings for a popular tune. The grouping of similar variations and the overlapping of variation styles suggests a meditation on this flexible subject, progressing less along a predetermined outline than by associative connections: the theme comes to its appointed end, but the improvising composer-performer continues exploring the same dimension of possibilities evoked by the variation just concluded. Or a new possibility strikes him for the second half of the theme, which he continues to work with as the theme begins again. The result is a leisurely con-

27. Hilda Andrews, in the preface to her edition of the Nevell book, draws attention to the free handling of voices in Byrd's keyboard counterpoint.

EXAMPLE 10

tinuous transformation of the eight-bar gestalt—always, the
first few notes of the tune are allowed recognition, but the
transition from the eighth to the first bar is without pause,
using an anacrusis as a bridge, or with an unemphatic cadence.
It often seems that there is no positive effort to link the variations locally; rather, the progressive unfolding of the theme
and of its musical possibilities is carried out in phases longer
than the eight-bar section, under the guidance of the composer's thought focused on those possibilities, not on the theme
as such nor on the arsenal of variation methods, nor perhaps
even on an eventual climax. The needed variety of pace and
texture occurs between the longer phases, but I do not think
there is any attempt to build the entire work into one grand
climactic sweep. The means of progression is scarcely even
comparative, but is an associative continuity so completely
integral that it is taken for granted. As with the motet, our
part is to accept the progressive transformations as they occur.
Retrospective shape is organized but irregular; like our other
examples, the set resists being neatly tied up in a visualizable
package.[28] Closure provided by the terminal heightening is

28. Cf. Nelson on Elizabethan variations generally: "The theme is followed by a moderate number of units, set off by cadences, which are arranged more or less progressively according to their rhythmic animation
and degree of figural elaboration. The growth in animation is not always
steady, being interrupted from time to time by a return to quieter rhythms,
yet by and large there is a noticeable increase in activity from the beginning of a set to the end. Aside from this somewhat desultory scheme of
growth, the ordering of the separate variations is indefinite, for despite the
frequent appearance of isolated pairs, more systematic groupings are rare"
(pp. 31–32). And on Byrd's *Walsingham,* variations 11 and 12: "Whether
the figuration is derived from the cantus firmus or is independent of it,
a figure introduced at the outset of a variation does not, as a rule, persist
throughout. Instead, the common plan is for a variation to present a succession of figures, one giving way to the next at a point of structural cleav-
age, or even, for no seeming reason, during the course of a phrase. Sometimes the figures used in the later course of a variation are no more than
variants of the one employed initially; at other times the later figures are
distinctly new. . . . A possible reason for this figural diversity is the apparent desire on the part of composers of cantus firmus variations to se-
cure, within the separate variations, internal variety and plasticity" (p. 37).

effective in the progressive mode only—a remark that we found
applies also to the dance that concludes *Gallathea.*

   Not every one of Byrd's variation sets shows all of the same
features as *Walsingham,* but many do—especially the longer
sets like *The Carman's Whistle, Will you walk the woods so
wild, Sellinger's Round,* and the perhaps later (because not
in the Nevell book) *John come kiss me now.*[29] Certain habits
of construction amount almost to marks of Byrd's authorship:
the refusal to make the use of a single variation style coincide
in extent with the length of the theme, and the stress on moment-to-moment continuity. More often than not, the theme
is identified upon its recurrences by its first few notes, and all
cadences except the last are treated as incidental. These two
characteristics result in a shift of the perceived sectional boundaries from the end to the beginning of the theme, reminiscent
of the motet's many begun but few concluded phrases; and as
a corollary they result in a weakening of the subclimaxes made
available by the typically climactic (because more strongly
tonal) shape of the folk tunes. Less ambitious sets—those that
seem designed rather to enhance the melody than to exploit its
musical possibilities—are more apt to let the segmental divisions remain clear, and even to reinforce the divisions by using
the cadence as an opportunity to change styles. The best examples of this type of set come from sources other than the
Nevell book. If that means that these sets are later compositions, it may well be that the ayre settings coincide with the
renewed interest in accompanied solo song about the time of
the publication of Dowland's *First Book of Ayres* in 1597. *O
mistress mine,* on which Byrd wrote one of his most engaging
sets, first appeared in 1599 in Morley's *First Book of Consort
Lessons.* Although Byrd avoided the madrigal fad of the 1590s
and later, the song variations along with his secular songs may
represent his way of responding to a change in musical fashion.
   Despite Byrd's preference in the more composerly sets for

29. *Fitz,* 1:214, 263, 248, 47; Byrd, *Works,* 20:7, 53, 47, 31.

linear continuity, variations are of course fundamentally a segmental form. The other subgenre, the dance variation, is somewhat less amenable to fantasylike treatment in the manner of
Walsingham, and is more restricted in its conventionally de-
creed procedure than are variations on song tunes, as the connection with prescribed patterns of dance movements would
lead us to expect. All of the dance forms, from the stateliest
pavan to the slightest coranto, have one feature in common:
the melody is divided into two or more strains, each of which
may be varied immediately after its appearance. In the tiniest
examples, like Byrd's one extant jig, the source may give simply the two strains, without any written variations at all. Almost certainly the performer would improvise a variation for
each. In a longer piece such as *Monsieur's Alman* or *The
Queen's Alman* the two strains might not only be varied after
their first statement, but brought back for further variations,
always in the order of initial presentation.[30] The pavan and
galliard, usually paired together as a kind of two movement
suite, both generally consisted of three strains, each varied once
in turn. There are not, to my knowledge, any examples of
these dances in which further variations take place, though a
composer might make another dance based on the same material further elaborated, and entitle it *Variatio.* The pavan
and galliard are thus structurally parallel, each having the
outline $A_1 A_2 B_1 B_2 C_1 C_2$; the duple rhythm of the pavan
and the triple rhythm of the galliard supply a ready-made
contrast between halves of the pair, though it should be remembered that the main contrast was in the dance steps, not
in the music.[31] It was possible but not obligatory to use the
same melody, suitably altered, for the galliard as for the pavan;
where this occurs, the link between the two pieces is obviously
strengthened.

The more modest song variations, for example *Callino Casturame (Fitz,* 2:186), begin with a simple exposition; the second section supplies passing notes and some rhythmic punc-

30. *Fitz,* 1:234 and 2:217; Byrd, *Works,* 18:79 and 90.
31. Donington, pp. 330–31.

tuation; later variations may use a few imitative points or rapid passages. There is in the later sets a tendency for variations to become more complex as they succeed each other, a development that challenges both performer and listener, and sustains interest. A typical pavan or galliard proceeds very differently from this. In the first place, the subject is not usually a familiar tune; the *subject*, to be precise, is the entire sixteen- or eight-bar segment, including all counterpoint and ornamentation. The reprise is nearly always more rapid, and it is established from the outset as a separate section, analogous to the first but not a mirror of it. The continuity of the theme throughout first, third, and fifth sections is apt to be hypothetical rather than a really heard relationship. These sections are effectively only related by key and style, except when a familiar tune (like *Flow my tears*) is used. In some of the lighter forms, the coranto for instance, the strains may be more obviously continuous; but all sorts of dance variations show clearer sectional divisions than do the more elaborate song settings. They are in this respect closer kin to the simpler variations on popular songs. Of Byrd's pavans and galliards, those in the Nevell book show by and large somewhat less decisive sectional differentiation, and are less likely to employ one style throughout a section than are presumably later examples. A comparison of the so-called first pavan and galliard in Nevell with the pavan and galliard "in A re" would illustrate this difference,[32] which will be discussed further in relation to the younger generation of composers.

The peculiar interaction of fundamentally segmented forms with a predominant stress on associative continuity, of alternation that suggests symmetry with what seems a disregard of the retrospective mode in which symmetry is most effective—such paradoxes as these have sometimes made serial works of the 1580s seem to a modern observer like inept or inchoate versions of the more easily definable forms that emerge in the

32. Byrd, *Works*, 19:1 and 94.

following decade. The quality hardest to grasp of the earlier works, the one that makes them seem vague, rambling, uncertain, is the artists' taking for granted things that the next musical generation felt compelled to demonstrate. Succeeding sections could in the earlier phase be allowed to cohere with each other by letting time-honored habits of composition or the practical effects of staging take their course; no elaborate system of intersegmental linking by means of recurrent elements or explicit transitions was necessary. Again, the primary concern with sequential arrangement, and that at the local level, resulted in what often seem to us muffled climaxes and a failure of retrospective unity. The most recent approach to these puzzling phenomena, at least from the literary side, seems to be an insistence on the complexity of the forms, opposed to the oversimplified schema that our passion for unity has sometimes led us to impose.[33] I would suggest, however, on the basis of the preceding discussion, that the real problem is—if I may put it so—more subtle than complexity. The artists of the 1580s were still able to work in familiar modes that everyone who mattered was presumed to understand intuitively. Only as these modes (one example of which is, literally, the modes in music) ceased to be unconscious assumptions was it felt necessary to ensure the recognition of form by the more blatant devices of comparison, climax, and recurrence.

33. This newer view is represented by Lindheim; Bevington; D. S. Brewer, "The hoole book," in *Essays on Malory*, pp. 41–63; and Catherine Lord, "Unity with Impunity," *Journal of Aesthetics and Art Criticism* 26 (1967): 103–06.

5

Coherence and Contrast

All of the examples disussed so far have been segmental forms.
Their foundation is a series of discrete parts, proceeding in
order: first this, then that, then a third thing. The segmental
framework is in every case modified, though to varying degrees, by forces that make for continuity. *Gallathea* and Byrd's
later variation sets show their segmental basis most clearly; in
Civitas sancti tui, the *Arcadia,* and *Campaspe,* the borders of
segments are smoothed over, chiefly by systems of overlapping,
but also by associative links between nonadjacent parts. Byrd's
Walsingham variations partake of both the segmental and the
continuous characteristics in something like equal proportions.
From this point there are two main lines of development:
segmental forms that show a particular concern for intersegmental organization, and continuous forms that show a particular concern for the distribution and control of expectation.
The latter represent changing preferences in directional models, changes tending toward the inclusive climactic crescendo
which in its innumerable guises has been the favorite form
in Western art from Biblical days to our own. The end of the
sixteenth century is only one of the periods in history when
a new development of climactic form occurred. In this instance
the climactic form exercised its magnetic attraction upon most
poets and composers, but not on all, not with equal force, and
not on everyone at the same time. The trend is toward it, but
even people who are going in the same general direction do
not necessarily reach the exact same place at the same moment.
That is why too rigid an adherence to the notion of periods
in the history of art inevitably leads to distortion; the phe-

nomena must define the period, as well as the other way
around.

The trend toward climactic forms is easy to see, and it has
been examined time and again from many angles. The internal
developments in the segmental forms are less easy to see, mainly
because they almost never take place apart from the other,
directional, development. But that does not mean the less
spectacular kinds of change are insignificant; on the contrary,
if we ignore them, we cannot help misinterpreting certain
works. It is not a simple matter of form *A* being superseded
by form *B*, but an interaction between the adoption of new
fashions and the modification of old ones. All the examples
that follow show more or less plainly the pull of the climactic
model, a fact that we are not likely to overlook, and one that
will be dealt with in its own right in chapter 6. For the time
being we may take that for granted, in order to free our attention for making other discernments.

John Bull was one of the most admired keyboard virtuosos
of his day. His music has since suffered an eclipse, though
every now and then someone has tried to remind us that most
of Bull's works are neither dry pedantic studies nor flashy dis-
plays without depth; perhaps the recordings of some of his
pieces during the last few years may help to restore Bull to
his rightful position among Elizabethan composers.[1] The work
by Bull that we are to bring under scrutiny is a set of variations on *Have with you to Walsingham* (*MB,* 19:46; *Fitz,* 1:1),
the same tune that provided Byrd with a norm for the set discussed in chapter 4. We know that Byrd's set was written be-

1. The most thorough critique of Bull's *oeuvre* is Wilfrid Mellers's pair
of articles, "John Bull and English Keyboard Music," *Music Quarterly* 40
(1954): 364–83 and 548–71. See also the note on the Bull example in Archibald T. Davison and Willi Apel, eds., *Historical Anthology of Music;* p.
178; Hugh Miller, "John Bull's Organ Works," *Music and Letters* 28
(1947): 25–35; and the brief preface to *MB* 14 and 19. For recordings, see
discography.

fore 1591, but of the date of Bull's *Walsingham* there is scarcely a clue.[2] Bull was born in 1562, and died in the Netherlands in 1628. Beyond an impression that the *Walsingham* variations are the work of a mature composer, we cannot date them; as an example of serial design, however, Bull's variations belong quite definitely to a later historical moment than Byrd's. Van den Borren observed that Bull's set also shows a more advanced sense of tonality, a point confirmed by Wilfrid Mellers; since this implies climactic order within each segment, it is further evidence of two kinds of formal change that I shall try to describe.[3]

A cursory glance at Example 11 suggests that Bull was copying Byrd's model: a single voice has the opening lead, the first and last variations are polyphonic, and the first five variations are grouped together by similar texture. But there the resemblance ends, if indeed it goes so far. Bull's opening variation is a more conventional imitative point; voices enter in descending order—in "logical order," we might almost say—keeping always close together, and until the eighth bar avoiding the lower range of the keyboard. Bull scarcely pauses at the first full cadence, but moves immediately in the second variation to a rhythmic intricacy comparable to Byrd's twentieth. By the third variation there can be no mistake about the keyboard orientation of Bull's polyphony, as the broken octaves for the left hand in bar 21 fulfill a hint given in bar 7. Nevertheless, this is to be an ambitious work, similar to Byrd's in its great length proportionate to the snippet of theme, and the composer can afford to take his time. Not until the sixth variation does Bull introduce a rapid figure, and even then the figure used is related to the little flourish of the lone upper voice in the second bar. From the sixth variation on, Bull brings into play every imaginable technical resource. Triple rhythms, arpeggios, repeated notes, dotted figures, cross-

2. Mellers, "John Bull and English Keyboard Music," p. 561; *MB* 19, preface; van den Borren, p. 224.

3. Van den Borren, p. 222; Mellers, "John Bull and English Keyboard Music," pp. 562–63. All musical examples are from *MB* 19:46–59.

EXAMPLE 11

rhythms, crossed hands—every variation shows something different. The virtuosity is carried to the point where the theme
appears to have become nothing but a given length of eight
bars, into each recurrence of which some new figuration is put.
There is some justice in this impression, since Bull does take the
length of the theme as a limit for the type of figuration used,
much more consistently than Byrd had done. A glance through
the printed scores will make this plain: even visually, Bull's
variations show a series of discrete patterns, each contained
between two of the periodic double bars. Both composers were
thinking in segmental terms, but for Bull the segment is a
separate and self-enclosed entity to be compared with adjacent
segments, not the flexible rhythmic pulse that it was for Byrd.

    As the segments have become more individualized, so the
points of their conjunction have become the critical moments
in the progressive form. The cyclical recurrence of the theme

is not a simple fact any more; something definite has to be done about it. Two kinds of things, generally speaking, are available: either the segments can be deliberately and explicitly linked together by consecutive or nonconsecutive means; or the figuration of successive segments can be so chosen as to emphasize their disjunction by means of contrast. Both linking and contrast, whether they occur together or at different times, invite comparison between the segments. In Bull's procedure, contrast is often the outstanding method, as for example between variations 5 and 6; 9, 10, and 11; 18 and 19; 27 and 28; and 29 and 30. The tenth variation, with its interplay of the hands, is set apart from those on either side of it, both of which depend on more rapid continuous figures; the twentieth introduces triple rhythm; the twenty-fifth involves a little hopping figure in startling contrast to the sextolets just preceding it; and the return of polyphonic texture in the last variation marks it off as definitely as possible from the virginalistic techniques used in the greater part of the set. These are only some of the most obvious cases, in a work where differences are highlighted throughout. Any pair of successive variations taken at random will show the same principle of comparative progression at work, often by shifting the more rapid line of figuration from one hand to the other (14-15-16, 22-23-24), or by making a special point of the cadence (8, 15, 16, 17, 24).

The danger with this disjunctive method is that it may succeed too well, and the piece of music may become a sequence of unrelated fragments. I do not think Bull allows this to happen. One reason for looking at such relatively long works is that in the absence of a vocal text, the composer must put all his reliance on an unsupported musical design, and the difficulty of doing this for more than a very few minutes (especially in an age when vocal music provided most of the formal conventions) puts the composer's formal strategy on display. Needless to say, the performer is on exhibition too, and to play Bull's *Walsingham* variations right through would perhaps not ordinarily be practical. But the outlines of a structure embracing the entire set are strong enough to make uncut perform-

ance intelligible, even though the structure is not, as I understand it, a sort of disembodied geometric shape, but a coherent
process, in constant interaction with the disjunctive forces mentioned above.

The cadences, again, are crucial: how are all the variations
through the twenty-ninth kept from being final? How, after
some impressive moment, is the continuation of the set kept
from being anticlimactic? A few local examples will begin to
indicate what Bull was doing. Variations 2, 14, 20, and 23 make
a point of running over the cadence by reducing the length
of the final chord and using the last beat or two of the last
measure of one variation as an anacrusis to the variation that
comes next, as in Example 12. Often this simple and effective
end-to-end linking joins together segments that are *dis*joined
by either a contrast or a shift of range in their characteristic
figuration. In fact the ordinary cadence, with its broken chord

EXAMPLE 12

EXAMPLE 12—(*Continued*)

(at least to the point of a reiterated tonic A) is ambiguous, since the figure shown in Example 13 can be taken either as an emphatic ending or as a lead into the opening notes of the next segment, making the most of the common A and E to counteract the necessarily abrupt shift from C-sharp to C-natural. Nonconsecutive links, though often less explicit, are present in abundance. I have already mentioned that the characteristic figure of the sixth variation picks up a conspicuously placed flourish near the beginning of the piece. Such opportu-

EXAMPLE 13

nities for recognition naturally become easier to arrange as more of the music is behind us, so that scattered similarities, like those in Example 14, become noticeable.

The twenty-eighth and twenty-ninth variations, though in no sense a recapitulation, offer a summary of figures from many of the preceding segments—a summary that is certainly not the last resource of wearied invention, if the surprises that meet us at strategic points throughout the set are any measure of Bull's fertility. There is a careful balance between the development of previously introduced motives and the introduction of new ones. Here and there a segment will stand alone,

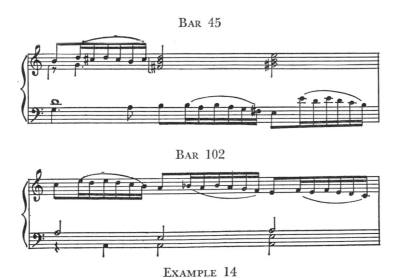

BAR 45

BAR 102

EXAMPLE 14

EXAMPLE 14—(*Continued*)

like numbers 6, 10, and 19; more often segments are grouped
in twos and threes by related material. The most decisive cadences followed by contrast do not come in the first half of
the set at all, but seem placed so as to forestall fatigue just
where they are least expected and most needed, closing variations 15, 24, and 29. Also late in the set for the most part are
internal changes of figuration within a segment. These occur
conspicuously in variations 28 and 29, but in several other
instances from the twelfth variation on. The twelfth variation
itself provides a final example of how Bull maintains continuity. It begins with the broken chords for both hands simultaneously quoted in Example 14—not Bull's most difficult technical device, but surely one of the most sonorous—which seems
the logical climactic outcome of variation 11. But after less
than two bars the upper part condenses to block chords, and
the figures are gradually transformed and slowed down until a
succeeding variation is not only possible but necessary. To close
the set Bull makes use of a generalized backward reference, this
time fulfilling the "law of return" by reintroducing the intricate polyphonic texture that has been scarcely more than
hinted at since the first unit of five variations. With its return,
the full circle is consummated.

The dual operation of contrast and coherence that gives
shape to Bull's *Walsingham* variations can be seen in other
musical genres, too. The tendency in the fantasia for viol consort, for instance, is for the succession of independent but overlapping "points" (the fantasia by John Munday partly quoted
in Example 5 is a classic illustration of this procedure until
about halfway to the end) to develop in two directions: first,
each motif is worked out at more length, so as to form the
structural basis of a large section of the work; and second,
these larger sections are arranged to contrast in theme and
texture with each other. This variety of form, consisting of a
few large contrasting sections, each more tightly coherent internally than was to be expected in the earlier sort of fantasia,
can already be found in a few works of William Byrd; the
fantasias of William Lawes in the mid-seventeenth century
show the development at a fully mature stage. The change in

the shape of the fantasia is in terms of serial form closely related to the growing preference in variation sets for one dis-
tinctive figuration from beginning to end of each segment (or
in a large work a group of segments), and to confine a given
characteristic to the limits marked by the length of the theme.
In sets by younger composers, like Gibbons and Farnaby, the
preference for internal consistency within the segment and
contrast between segments is clearly evident.[4]

The drama has a certain affinity with these musical forms
in that ordinarily only one kind of action happens at one time;
that is, where different groups of characters are involved—the
two parts of *Henry IV* will serve as a reference point for the
moment—only one group is allowed to hold the stage, and
this group must go off to give place to a different group. No
matter how neatly the exits and entrances are managed, the
succession of more or less enclosed segments of action is an
inescapable fact. Any one of dozens of Elizabethan plays might
serve as our example here: Greene's *Friar Bacon* and *James
IV*, Kyd's *Spanish Tragedy*, Jonson's early and middle comedies, the composite *Life of Sir John Oldcastle*, and so on and
on. A sufficiently clear instance, and one whose mildly proble-
matical structure may be illuminated by an examination in
terms of serial form, is Shakespeare's *Merchant of Venice*, first
acted in 1596–98, and printed in 1600.[5]

It will be remembered that in both the comedies of Lyly
discussed in the preceding chapter, there was evidence of the
use of multiple staging. The court, the painter's studio, and
Diogenes's tub in *Campaspe* seem to be fixed subareas on the
stage, and the symbolic central oak of *Gallathea* was probably
in place throughout the play, being adverted to or not as the
action of each scene required. In later plays, including *The
Merchant of Venice*, this medieval method has been replaced

4. See *MB* 20 (Gibbons) and 24 (Farnaby). Few of Gibbons's works appear
in *Fitz*; all of Farnaby's do, but they are scattered through the two volumes.
5. All references are to the *New Arden Shakespeare* text, by act and
scene.

by a convention whereby the whole stage becomes different places for different bits of action. If the number of places is limited and the action returns to a place previously localized, the imaginary places become permanent for the duration of the play. Thus in contrast to, say, the first part of *Tamburlaine,* in which there is a succession of places without a return to any of them, Shakespeare limits his action to two or three locales, in this case to Venice and Belmont. *The Merchant* is of course not the first English play to do this, but it is obvious that such use of the "law of return" effects a great gain in coherence—the art of making separate parts of a work stick together. Any type of recurrence operates to enhance our impression of simultaneity in a serial work, and thereby contributes to the shaping of a simple, consistent form in the retrospective mode of perception. In the progressive mode, however, recurrence needs special handling if it is to ensure coherence. Consider what would happen if Bassanio stayed in Venice, and Portia's lucky suitor were some character whom we never saw except at Belmont. Some kind of linking is essential, and the most easily available kind in drama is to have a character play an important part in both places. As in narrative, the smoothest way to move from place to place, from episode to episode, is to move with a character. In formal terms, Bassanio and Portia are not persons who make journeys, but recurrent elements whose appearance in different contexts serves to link the contexts together. The extreme case of such linking would be the *liaison de scènes* that keeps a single character on stage while one group with whom he is connected goes off and a second group enters (see, for instance, Chapman, *The Conspiracy of Byron,* act 1, scene 2). But to go to that extreme is to sacrifice to continuity the value of contrasting settings: if one person remains stationary before us, the dramatist cannot make us believe that the locus of action has changed. The implied commentary of places on one another is for Shakespeare a fundamental technique, not to be abandoned even for the sake of coherence.

The fact that climactic development is so unmistakably the

governing directional model in *The Merchant of Venice* makes
it less convincing to talk about the local interrelation of segments than it was in our earlier examples; any of the Henry
VI plays, for instance, would provide easier material. But it
is important to see that even in a climactic play of around 1600,
comparative progression in the segmental aspect of form is
being dealt with to some extent in its own right; to reduce
every element and every segment to a place in the climactic
curve is, I think, to do the play an injustice. The first four
scenes of act 1, then, alternate between Venice and Belmont.
The second and fourth scenes, along with act 2, scenes 7 and
9, do not constitute a subplot, properly speaking, since the
fairy-tale device of the rich maiden and the three caskets is
something we know all about beforehand; that story is simply
waiting for Bassanio to come and finish it off by making the
right choice. Not for a moment do we expect Morocco or Ar-
ragon to open the leaden casket. Further, there is no simultaneous movement from Belmont to Venice, nor is there any
deadline for Bassanio to meet, or preliminary ordeals for him
to undergo; the only delaying complication is financial, and
that, until 3.2, belongs entirely to the Venetian scene. Meanwhile, Portia is waiting with as much patience as reason could
ask.[6] The shift of scene, characters, and language from 1.1 to
1.2 is designedly abrupt, despite the preparation given us by
Bassanio's comparison of Portia's sunny locks to the golden
fleece. Scene 1 moves through several kinds and degrees of male
companionship; scene 2 presents only women. The prose of
the two speaking parts, Portia and Nerissa, is set against the
rich allusions and earnest sentiment of Bassanio's and Antonio's verse. There is nothing so urgent in the speech of the
ladies; at most their wit reflects a restless tedium that Portia
beguiles by the set-pieces describing her sundry wooers. Nerissa's reference to Bassanio complements Bassanio's praise of

6. Much of Granville-Barker's preface to this play still makes good sense,
especially the comments on Portia and on the meshing of the two stories
(*Prefaces to Shakespeare,* 4:88–119).

Portia in linking scene 2 back to the main plot already set afoot in Venice; in another direction, the arrival of the prince of Morocco is announced, so that we can look forward with some interest to the next scene at Belmont.

The easily flowing prose that Portia and Nerissa exchange serves in its turn for a background against which Shylock's abrupt short lines at the beginning of scene 3, with their hesitant rhythms and cautious reiterations, stand out the more sharply:[7]

> If I could bid the fifth welcome with so good heart as I can bid the other four farewell, I should be glad of his approach: if he have the condition of a saint, and the complexion of a devil, I had rather he should shrive me than wive me.
>
> . . . . . .
>
> Three thousand ducats, well.
>
> . . . .
>
> For three months, well.
>
> . . . .
>
> Antonio shall become bound, well.

This return to Venice of course furthers the plot from the point at which we left it at the end of scene 1; but it also shows us a new side of Venetian society—the sordidness, mixed with Old Testament practicality, of Shylock's concerns, as against the idealizing and ennobling fellow-feeling of Antonio and his friends. Scene 3 closes with these contrasting tones in apposition: the inscrutable Shylock covers his real thoughts by attending to the safety of his house; Bassanio is uneasy about the "merry bond" on which his love venture depends, and Antonio high-mindedly refuses to worry. Immediately in act 2, scene 1 all these developing moods are countered by the exotic magnificence of the tawny prince "all in white," accompanied

7. C. L. Barber, *Shakespeare's Festive Comedy,* pp. 172–73 and 181–82. Barber interprets Shylock's style here as a reduction of humanity to reflexes, and compares *Richard II,* 3. 2. 175–76.

by a train of followers. The sudden focus on the visible, after
our concern with evaluating hidden intentions, is matched by
the elevated ritual of Morocco's gallant protestations:

> *Shy.* Then meet me forthwith at the notary's
> Give him direction for this merry bond—
> And I will go and purse the ducats straight,
> See to my house left in the fearful guard
> Of an unthrifty knave: and presently
> I'll be with you.
> *Ant.*   Hie thee gentle Jew.
> The Hebrew will turn Christian, he grows kind.
> *Bass.* I like not fair terms, and a villain's mind.
> *Ant.* Come on, in this there can be no dismay,
> My ships come home a month before the day.
>
> [1.3]

> *Mor.* Mislike me not for my complexion,
> The shadowed livery of the burnish'd sun,
> To whom I am a neighbor, and near bred.
> Bring me the fairest creature northward born,
> Where Phoebus' fire scarce thaws the icicles,
> And let us make incision for your love,
> To prove whose blood is reddest, his or mine.
>
> [2.1]

As scene 3 offered departures from both the immediately preceding scene 2 and from the first scene in Venice, so here the
opulent high style contrasts with the previous Belmont scene's
casual talk as well as with the combination of inwardness and
practicality that ends scene 3. One could go on comparing segments in this way—Launcelot's "Certainly, my conscience will
serve me to run from this Jew my master . . ." follows directly
upon Morocco's "Good fortune then, To make me blest or
cursed'st among men!"—but the principle is sufficiently clear.

As we leave Belmont the second time, Morocco is just preparing to try his luck (or wisdom) with the three caskets; the
moment of his choice does not come until appreciably later,

after Jessica's elopement. But the principles of alternation and contrast are not therefore left in abeyance. The second scene of act 2 is the clown's scene; in 2.3 Launcelot turns our attention to the "gentle" Jessica, and she directs us to Lorenzo and the elopement conspiracy. These anxious plans are carried out only after a renewed glimpse of Shylock's miserly malice, this time interacting with the parodic fooling of Launcelot. In fact, this portion of the play, although it also includes characters belonging to the main plot, establishes a subsidiary group of contrasts between the fools and the lovers until the primary scheme is resumed with Morocco's choice in 2.7. The methods of alternation and of a continuity maintained by carefully leaving off incompleted actions (this occurs more commonly in the latter part of the play, whereas links of character and reference are more usual in the earlier scenes) are closely related to the methods of Sidney's narrative. By the end of act 2 Shakespeare has set enough different lines in motion for every scene to end with the suspenseful incompletion of one or another of them. The way Shakespeare handles this technique of maintaining continuity does, however, show an important difference from the techniques of earlier artists, in that the comparative progression is also a teleological one.

Act 5, the final gathering at Belmont, is usually explicated along thematic lines; that is, the scene is relevant and not anticlimatic because it "expresses a tendency in society and nature which supports life and expels what would destroy it." [8] In the concluding contretemps with the rings "the group provides one final demonstration that human relationships are stronger than their outward signs"; and anyhow the rings "are all that remain of the plot to keep the play moving after the trial"—that is, the only unresolved ambiguity in the action. We might add that the rings do not, strictly speaking, "remain," since the business centered on them is not introduced until the trial is over, as an only too obvious device to lend specificity to our expectation of the last scene; as a device, in short, for linking

8. Barber, p. 189; immediately following quotes are from pp. 187 and 186.

the return to Belmont with the trial. As a recurrent motif, first
ambiguously open-ended, then in the last lines of the play completed, the exchange of rings serves its purpose; it also saves
the initial exchange in 3.2 from being an irrelevant piece of
sentiment. Why, though, as a matter of form, is the return to
Belmont needed at all? We saw that the concluding dance in
Gallathea functions simultaneously as epilogue, summary and
terminal heightening; act 5 of *The Merchant of Venice* appears to serve much the same purposes. Only as terminal
heightening is this function questionable, since the trial scene
is clearly the climax of the plot, whereas act 5 is related to
the preceding action primarily by contrast. The principles of
alternation and return make a final scene at Belmont desirable
in order to achieve a sense of balance or symmetry which would
otherwise be difficult for the playgoer to apprehend so fully.
By this last grand alternation between the two milieus, Shakespeare casts over the play as a whole the retrospective impression of a more regular to and fro movement than the play in
progress up to this point could have given us.

The ring business, as we saw, provides a superficial if unmistakable link with the posttrial scene, but there is a more
effective and more subtle comparative tactic that ensures firm
cohesion. At the end of act 4, after the intense concentration
on the precise meaning of words that has marked the trial, the
lovers and their disguised ladies exchanged arguments in po-
lite competition and, on the lovers' side, in real confusion.
Portia in demanding the ring was manipulating Bassanio, taking advantage of his ignorance of her identity in order to
overcome him in a lovers' game—another sort of "merry bond."
Jessica and Lorenzo follow these intricate cross-purposes with
the play's most thoroughly cooperative dialogue, a formal exchange of comparisons, competitive only in the desire to enhance further the happy couple's mutual delight. As Lorenzo's
speeches on celestial harmony affirm the society based on love
that had been negatively demonstrated in the defeat of Shylock, so this cooperative game is a contrasting analogue to the
unmutual communications of Portia and Bassanio. We do not

have to wait for the subject of the rings to be brought up again before we can understand the relevance of the final scene: it is given us from the outset by Shakespeare's artifice of a contrast that is in itself a powerful means of coherence.

Caroline Spurgeon remarked that she could not find "any continuous symbol in the images" of *The Merchant of Venice*, although the comparisons of Shylock to a dog and a wolf (1.3. 111 and 116; and 4.1. 90–93 and 133) seemed to give "the key to the whole action."[9] If we were determined to find some instance of verbal recurrence, the word "gentle" might be a good one to pursue; but recurrent words and images were perhaps not needed in a play that bases its form on the recurrence of much larger units. They are, however, a determinant of coherence in many works, especially where the total form is experimental or potentially discontinuous—the occasionally echoed motives in Bull's *Walsingham* variations are a modest case in point. A more thoroughgoing example, this time in nondramatic poetry, of reliance on irregular recurrence is Spenser's *Fowre Hymnes*.[10] Unlike our two preceding examples, this is a radically segmental work; although the hymns are best taken together as Spenser intended them to be, each hymn can stand alone, apart from the tetrad to which it belongs. Separately and together the hymns have inspired some confusion in their critics, a confusion that may be due to Spenser's employing means of serial organization that are not entirely consistent with each other.

Spenser's protest in the dedication to the *Fowre Hymnes* that he intends the second pair as a corrective to the first leads us to expect a greater degree of contrast between the pairs than in fact there is.[11] The contrast is topical, not formal; the for-

9. *Shakespeare's Imagery and What It Tells Us*, p. 285.

10. All references are to *The Works of Edmund Spenser: A Variorum Edition*, vol. 1, *The Minor Poems*. I am indebted to the notes in this edition and to W. L. Renwick, ed., *Daphnaida and Other Poems*, pp. 209 ff., 373–77; William Nelson, *The Poetry of Edmund Spenser*, pp. 97–115; and Thomas P. Roche, Jr., *The Kindly Flame*, pp. 124–25.

11. See the full discussion of the problem of dating the first two hymns by Robert Ellrodt, *Neoplatonism in the Poetry of Spenser*, pp. 14–23. Ell-

mal relations between the hymns are mostly analogic similarities. If we take each of the hymns as a segment, they are held together by much the same means as the stanzas of *Aske me no more*, that is, by the use of the same directional model for each segment. The model is similar to the climactic, but it does not consist of a single smooth rising curve, every point along which contributes to one culminating moment. Rather, it is made up of a rise, a drop, and a second rise. For instance, *An Hymne in Honour of Love* begins with an invocation addressed to the subject of the poem, then launches upon a Creation myth that leads to the exaltation of human love, culminating in the affirmation, "For loue is Lord of truth and loialtie" (*HL*, l. 176). It is not a sharp peak—both the ascent to it and the descent from it are gradual and intermittent—but after this point the poet turns to a catalogue of lovers' feelings, mostly distresses, that merges into the second culmination, the vision of Love's paradise. *An Hymne in Honour of Beautie* similarly begins its first rise with cosmic considerations, progressing to the union of bodily and spiritual beauty (as in the first hymn there was the convergence of Love and man). The following stanzas descend to qualifications of that union, a procedure that, unlike the psychological observations in *Love*, has a debilitating effect on the vision of loveliness just passed. Spenser recovers power when he begins celebrating mutual love in the second rise, which is completed in the triumph of Venus. *An Hymne of Heavenly Love* once again tells a Creation story, the counterpart of the pagan version in *Love*. Here the climactic union is that of God and man in Christ. The second rise comes to the crucifixion from Christ's human side, and goes beyond it to the glory of contemplation. The double

---

rodt inclines to the view that the four poems were written to go together, not long before their publication, but he does not rule out the possibility that the first two were written earlier, then revised. Enid Welsford, in *Spenser: Fowre Hymnes and Epithalamion*, pp. 37–38, prefers this latter possibility, which seems the more likely to me also. But since I am not trying to give precise dates for the transformations in English poetry, this need not be an issue here.

climaxes in *An Hymne of Heavenly Beautie* have elicited some unfavorable criticism, perhaps because the process is clearest in this poem.[12] The contemplative, moving from earth through the seven heavens, loses himself in rapture: "Cease then my tongue . . ." (*HHB*, l. 106). After this there ought not to be anything else, or so we feel;[13] but Spenser goes on to the vision of Sapience and another ecstasy.

Evidently, then, there are some difficulties in the progressive mode of these works. Especially in the two *Beautie* hymns the recession from the first high point of emotion has an anticlimactic effect, and the same deflation occurs, less disastrously, in *Heavenly Love*. Why this should be so is apparent from the *Hymne of Love*. In this first member of the set there was also the possibility of anticlimax, in the shift from Love the creator to Love the tyrant; but since the latter aspect of Love is set forth in the beginning there is no problem in returning to it when the Creation story has reached man. The switchover in *Heavenly Love* from the divine to the human nature of Christ, though it is not prepared for early in the poem, nevertheless "works" emotionally because the poet can rely on traditional Christian doctrine to have given the necessary explanations in advance. But in the *Hymne of Beautie* all the emphasis is on the intimate relation of physical and spiritual, which leaves us wholly unprepared for the poet's denial of this relation in lines 141–61. The failure is one of logic—poetic logic, at least, as it is in *Heavenly Beautie* where the reasonable and traditional sequence of the ladder of contemplation is betrayed by the abrupt shift from mysticism to theology.

The magnificent conclusion of *Heavenly Beautie* and of the whole set of hymns goes a long way to relieve these various difficulties. Spenser is at his breathtaking best in opening and closing stanzas and at the climaxes. All four hymns give the impression of terminally heightened forms with a superim-

12. E.g. Lewis, *English Literature in the Sixteenth Century*, pp. 376–77; Renwick, p. 212.

13. See Lowry Nelson, Jr., "The Rhetoric of Ineffability: Towards a Definition of Mystical Poetry," *Comparative Literature* 8 (1956): 323–26.

posed climactic order that does not always tally with the more
basic organization. The latter often (especially in the first pair)
shows through as a continuous, varied sequence of topics similar to the continuous forms discussed in chapter 4. But over
against the inconsistencies of the progressive mode we must set
the powerful impression of balance created in the retrospective
mode by patterns of recurrence. The analogous directional
models of the hymns, even though they are arranged in order
of increasing sublimity, contribute less to the coherence of the
set than does the strategic recurrence of words and images. If
we take Spenser's prefatory statement at face value, we may
believe that he was experimenting at an early date with this
strategy as applied to a complementary pair of poems. The
relation of the first two hymns to each other would then appear as a smaller attempt at a scheme later developed on the
larger scale of *Fowre Hymnes,* much as Eliot's "Burnt Norton"
appears in retrospect as a sketch for the unified structure of
Four Quartets. Whatever the dates of the hymns, it is clear
that all four are involved in a complicated web of recurrent
elements.

Some of these elements are dictated by the topical contrasts
between love and heavenly love, beauty and heavenly beauty.
Love, for instance, is the kindling fire whose rage torments the
lover, and the "life-giuing fyre" whose burning moves the ani-
mals "to multiply the likeness of their kynd" (*HL,* ll. 65, 100).
For man, however, to whom there are "some sparks remaining
of that heauenly fyre" (*HL,* l. 106), love is destructive, piercing,
burning, consuming, a scornful tyrant delighting in the lover's
anguish. One wonders why a retractation was needed of a poem
that makes love appear so unpleasant; but of course the items
of description are common counters of Elizabethan love poetry.
Besides the fire of love, Spenser concentrates on love's tyranny.
A helpless child armed with borrowed light, Love as creator
nevertheless proceeds by using force, binding the elements with
"adamantine chaines." In the same spirit love tyrannizes over
wretched mortals, though the lover prefers to think of his pain
as purgatorial; once it is passed he will enter Love's paradise

of pleasure. The poet's conception of Love resides more in
these verbal devices than in an underlying argument, in the
suggestive power of words rather than in the logical procession
of ideas. When he turns to heavenly love, fire and flame are
conspicuously absent (except for the hellfire in *HHL*, l. 89)
until the very end of the poem when their meaning is presumably divinized by the identification of Love with Christ.
Then and only then can the poet safely reintroduce the terms
and speak of the

> deuouring great desire
> Of his deare selfe, that shall thy feeble brest
> Inflame with loue, and set thee all on fire
> With burning zeale. . . .
> [*HHL*, ll. 268–71]

Against the tyrannical earthly Love who makes his subjects his
prisoners, Christ redeems man from bondage by making *himself* "a most demisse And abiect thrall" (*HHL*, ll. 136–37). The
image of Christ "reuyld, disgrast, and foule abusd" is Spenser's
answer to that other image of the "imperious boy."

In the first part of the *Hymne of Heavenly Love* the Holy
Spirit is called "pure lampe of light," and the angels are "all
glistring glorious in their Makers light," since in heaven "dark-
nesse there appeareth neuer none" (*HHL*, ll. 43, 56, 73). The
clusters of words and images for light, besides contrasting with
Love's borrowed brightness, are vital links with both *Beautie*
hymns. Treating love as effect, Spenser turns in *An Hymne in
Honour of Beautie* to its cause, the "Mouther of loue," whom
the poet invokes to "vouchsafe with thy loue-kindling light,
T'illuminate my dim and dulled eyne" (*HB*, ll. 19–20). The
Cyprian queen is associated throughout with her star as the
source of that beauty which is light immortal. Along with light
both in thought and rhyme goes *sight*, the highest of the bodily
senses. The lover's eyes

> See more then any other eyes can see,
> Through mutuall receipt of beames bright,

> Which carrie priuie message to the spright,
> And to their eyes that inmost faire display,
> As plaine as light discouers dawning day
> [*HB*, ll. 234–38]

Coming after an account of how the lover transforms the beloved into "an heauenly beautie to his fancies will" (*HB*, l. 222) in his thoughts, we might expect "that inmost faire" to be the spiritual essence of beauty. But not so—it is the visible fairness of the lady. Like Love, beauty is a conqueror, but a more benign one, who spreads her "louely kingdome ouer all" (*HB*, l. 266).

If the *Hymne of Beautie* used light as its keyword, the *Hymne of Heavenly Beautie* uses almost nothing else. This beauty, too, kindles love, but now it is the "sparkling light / Of thine eternall Truth" (*HHB*, ll. 10–11) that the poet prays will illumine him. As the soul in contemplation ascends in order through the seven heavens to the divine presence, the poet's language becomes saturated with fiery brightness. In the second rise Sapience, too, is

> with gemmes and iewels gorgeously
> Adornd, that brighter then the starres appeare,
> And make her natiue brightnes seem more cleare
> [*HHB*, ll. 187–89]

The lusts of the flesh renounced, the poet looks at last to "that soueraine light, / From whose pure beams al perfect beauty springs" (*HHB*, ll. 295–96), and ends his song on the word and thought of *rest*. The contrast between love's fire and the fire of zeal, between Love the tyrant and Love the redeemer, and the continuity of mortal beauty's light that becomes a mere shadow to the light of heavenly beauty—these are the things that hold the poems together as a set. Local links between adjacent hymns help too, as when the lover at the end of the *Hymne of Beautie* begs his mistress to "restore a damned wight from death" (*HB*, l. 287), and the phrase becomes ironical, nearly blasphemous, in the context of the *Hymne of Heavenly Love*. The latter ends as the soul is transported

> With sweete enragement of celestiall loue,
> Kindled through sight of those faire things aboue
>
> > [*HHL*, ll. 286–87]

—at which point the *Hymne of Heavenly Beautie* begins:

> Rapt with the rage of mine own rauisht thought,
> Through contemplation of those goodly sights
>
> > [*HHB*, ll. 1–2]

To say that these artifices produce a verbal but not a logical unity is probably true, but we can be more precise. The poet has used analogous directional models and recurrent elements to create a convincingly whole retrospective form. It is only when we read through the poems repeatedly, in the hope of finding our total impression confirmed by an equally deft progressive organization, that the formal weaknesses appear— weaknesses primarily in the guidance of expectation. The glorious passages remain glorious, but their context does not always seem adequate to them. In Bull's variations and in *The Merchant of Venice* coherence and contrast operate mainly in the progressive mode, and retrospective symmetry is more suggested than achieved; in the *Fowre Hymnes* there is also a concern for progressive coherence, but only insofar as this can be effected through linking by recurrent elements, whereas the symmetrical retrospective pattern is basic.

The growing preference for more emphatic design in serial forms manifests itself in every genre that I have been able to investigate. Eventually the climactic model comes to dominate the progressive mode and symmetry to rule the retrospective mode; but there is a time, for a generation or so across the turn of the seventeenth century, when the process has reached different points in different works. In general, however, two stages follow in order: plays become tidier before they become teleologically organized; verse narrative becomes smoother before it becomes more pointed; the lyric introduces startling effects before these are made subservient to an ascending pro-

gression; dance variations develop symmetry and heightened
terminal sections at about the same time (so far as their uncertain chronology permits one to judge); the craze for solo
song follows that for the madrigal, while the madrigal follows
both the Tudor part-song and the solo with a polyphonic ac-
companiment of viols; the fantasy's many brief points expand
to a few large contrasting sections that come to have their own
internal climactic developments. We have seen how the intermediate stage appears in three different guises, and I think we
need add only one more to give segmental forms at this stage
their fair representation.

The Byrd motet discussed in chapter 4 was offered as a basis
of comparison with other musical examples; in *Civitas sancti
tui* it is clear that the texture is the structure. That is, the
deployment of voices in various groups and interrelationships
and in different kinds of counterpoint is Byrd's primary means
of conveying the sense of wholeness that the motet evokes so
beautifully. For the most part, vocal textures shift in much
the same way as Byrd's keyboard variation techniques shift:
by associative methods. One type of procedure leads to another
through affinities that are seldom easy to specify, but are almost
always grasped intuitively by the receptive listener. In keeping
with the tendency in other serial art forms to make the me-
chanics of structure more explicit, we find that the handling
of melody and texture in vocal polyphony by younger composers becomes definable to the conscious intellect to a degree
that in *Civitas sancti tui* it is not. For an example we shall
have to leap from Byrd's sacred work to a secular one by John
Wilbye. The reason for the leap is that in the years after 1580,
the Italian madrigal took England's musical life by storm.
Spurred by the publication in 1558 of Yonge's *Musica Trans-
alpina* and Thomas Morley's adaptations of Italian ballets and
canzonets from 1593, the best composers of vocal music around
the turn of the century (other than Byrd) gave their best efforts
to secular works. To explain this development in public taste
—and it is a development, not an abrupt change, since the
Italian madrigals had been circulating in manuscript for some

time before any were printed—is beyond the scope of this study; it will be enough if we can observe it accurately. The secular forms, historically, grew out of sacred ones, and the sacred works were in their turn modified under the influence of techniques evolved in secular vocal polyphony.[14]

Wilbye's *Ye that do live in pleasures* was first printed in 1609. The abundant use in it of contrasting textures seems at first perusal remote from Byrd's subtlety, but it represents a refinement over Wilbye's methods in his earlier (1598) madrigal collection. The main new thing about the madrigal as opposed to other sorts of vocal polyphony is the degree to which musical details are bound to the words of the text. The English composers who wrote madrigals in the 1590s and early 1600s copied nearly all their techniques from the great Italian madrigalists who preceded them. Many of these techniques have to do with word-setting; there is no better summary of them than Thomas Morley's:

> It followeth to show you how to dispose your music according to the nature of the words which you are therein to express, as whatsoever matter it be which you have in hand such a kind of music must you frame to it. You must therefore, if you have a grave matter, apply a grave kind of music to it; if a merry subject you must make your music also merry, for it will be a great absurdity to use a sad harmony to a merry matter or a merry harmony to a sad, lamentable, or tragical ditty. . . . If you would have your music signify hardness, cruelty, or other such affects you must cause the parts proceed in their motions without the half note, that is, you must cause them proceed by whole notes, sharp thirds, sharp sixths, and such like. . . . But when you would express a lamentable pas-

14. These facts are dealt with in standard histories, such as Cannon et al.; Richard L. Crocker, *A History of Musical Style;* and Gerald Abraham, ed., *The New Oxford History of Music,* vol. 4, *The Age of Humanism, 1540–1630.* The best study of the English madrigal is Kerman's (1962), but E. H. Fellowes, *The English Madrigal Composers,* is still useful. On the ecclesiastical side, Huray offers the most comprehensive treatment.

sion then must you use motions proceeding by half notes, flat thirds, and flat sixths, which of their nature are sweet, specially being taken in the true tune and natural air with discretion and judgement. . . .

Also if the subject be light you must cause your music go in motions which carry with them a celerity or quickness of time, as minims, crotchets, and quavers; if it be lamentable the notes must go in slow and heavy motions as semibreves, breves, and suchlike. . . . Moreover you must have a care that when your matter signifieth "ascending," "high," "heaven," and such like you make your music ascend; and by the contrary where your ditty speaketh of "descending," "lowness," "depth," "hell," and others such you must make your music descend. . . .

The light music hath been of late more deeply dived into so that there is no vanity which in it hath not been followed to the full; but the best kind of it is termed Madrigal. . . . If therefore you will compose in this kind you must possess yourself with an amorous humour (for in no composition shall you prove admirable except you put on and possess yourself wholly with that vein wherein you compose), so that you must in your music be wavering like the wind, sometime wanton, sometime drooping, sometime grave and staid, otherwhile effeminate.[15]

These musical symbols for verbal meanings are a distinguishing mark of the madrigal, and go a long way to account for its form; but there are other characteristics that we must not overlook. Once again I shall call upon Morley; note that in this earlier section of the *Plain and Easy Introduction* he reaches the same conclusion as in the quotation above, but by a different route (he has just given an example, without words, from a six-part madrigal):

If you mark this well you shall see that no point is long stayed upon, but once or twice driven through all the

15. Thomas Morley, *A Plain and Easy Introduction to Practical Music* (1597), pp. 290–91, 294.

parts, and sometimes reverted, and so to the close, then taking another; and that kind of handling is most esteemed in Madrigals. . . . Also in these compositions of six parts you must have an especial care of causing your parts to give place one to another, which you cannot do without restings; nor can you . . . cause them rest till they have expressed that part of the dittying which they have begun, and this is the cause that the parts of a Madrigal, either of five or six parts, go sometimes full, sometimes very single, sometimes jumping together, and sometimes quite contrary ways, like unto the passion which they express; for as you scholars say that love is full of hopes and fears so is the Madrigal, or lovers' music, full of diversity of passions and airs.[16]

The madrigal was not always "lovers' music," strictly speaking (witness Wilbye's *Happy, oh happy he* and Gibbons's *What is our life,* among other examples), but a "diversity of passions and airs" ranks with symbolic word-setting as a prime determinant of its form. *Ye that do live in pleasures* is a fair representative in this respect, as it is also in its cheerfulness. Not that the English composers avoided Petrarchan texts of the more lugubrious sort—a glance through the poems in a few volumes of *The English Madrigalists* would quickly correct such an impression—but on the whole the English seem to have preferred happy texts more often than did their Italian masters. As a result the English madrigals tend to make up in freshness and liveliness what they may lack in profundity.

Turning to *Ye that do live in pleasures,* the difference from Byrd's handling of five voices is apparent at once (see Ex. 15).[17] The opening, with quintus and altus together, is typical of Wilbye's habit of using a pair of inner voices against the two outer ones. When the words are repeated, the quintus is paired with the tenor, and all voices drop to what we would call D major. Although modern conceptions of tonality scarcely apply

16. Morley, p. 282.
17. John Wilbye, *Second Set of Madrigals* (1609), p. 154.

EXAMPLE 15

EXAMPLE 15—(*Continued*)

to this music (nor for that matter do the modes), there is a
definite feeling of our major mode throughout the first twenty-
five bars. This apparently suited Wilbye's idea of cheerful
music for cheerful words as well as it does ours. Whatever key
this first section may be in from time to time, it plainly comes
back to D major in bars 24–26, at exactly the right moment to
prepare a contrast with the equally clear minor harmony of
"Not clogged with earth or worldly cares." The tempo slows
down, too, the notes becoming longer and longer, with held
notes in more voices as worldly cares clog the music more
heavily. "Come sing this song" (bar 43) again presents decisive
contrast in every way: a bright C major, homophonic texture,
a return of the little figure associated with the lively opening
passages. No such things, however, will do when the text mentions that Amphion "now is dead" (bar 46); sure enough, the
cantus vanishes (to come in plaintively a few bars later, over
the three lower voices), and a slow descending phrase makes
appropriate use of semitones to lament poor Amphion. Imitative contrapuntal texture returns, this time with all five voices

engaged, when the text becomes more optimistic. A further experiment in texture, beginning at bar 68, sets the line "And let him triumph over death" to a lively musical phrase (the happy figure that first appeared in the third bar comes in again), given to two voices while the others provide a sustained background—quite possibly the latter represent death and the moving voices enact triumph. However that may be, the next line is set homophonically and so too is the last line, with all voices moving quickly together, in a final affirmation of C major.

Ye that do live in pleasures, like any number of madrigals from its period, shows precisely those patterns of contrast and coherence between sections that we have already noticed in other musical and poetic works. The contrasts are by now sufficiently evident; this aspect is perhaps even more striking when we read the music silently than when it is actually heard. As for coherence, there is the habitual overlapping, whereby one musical section is continued at the same time as the next is beginning. But there is another reason for the impression of wholeness, even of homogeneity, that this work produces in spite of its internal contrasts. The motif that I have referred to as being associated with cheerful passages is an instance of a recurrent element's helping to bind sections together. Even in Byrd's motet we found a certain family resemblance between musical phrases; but it would have been difficult to demonstrate this resemblance to someone who did not already sense it. Here, however, the resemblance is closer, and we can put our finger on it (see Ex. 16). These are only samples; many others occur, transposed or inverted, and in every voice part at one time or another. True to the character of nonconsecutive recurrence in general, the use of this motif has a decisive effect on the retrospective form of Wilbye's madrigal. To put it very simply, one's recollection groups sections into those that do and those that do not incorporate the motif. The pattern is enhanced by the fact that the sections in which the motif does not appear are also differentiated by the confluent factors

EXAMPLE 16

of slower tempo and minor mode. Although the words of the poem determine which kind of section will occur when, Wilbye evidently found it desirable to use a musical means of structure along with the verbal one.[18] The recurrence becomes doubly significant when we notice how the music is poised between two different kinds of conventional orientation—it is no longer modal, nor is it yet fixed in harmonic tonality. This is the kind of situation in which recurrence is most valuable in organizing serial form, because it is a method that can be perceived regardless of whether the sequence to which it gives shape proceeds along familiar lines or not.

The last few bars of *Ye that do live in pleasures* make a bow to convention by ending the work as it began, that is, without flats or sharps. I hesitate to name either a key or a mode, but an obedience to the law of return is unquestionably intended. Further, even though the dynamics markings in Fellowes's text are editorial, the full texture, almost unanimous movement,

18. See Kerman, *The Elizabethan Madrigal,* pp. 239–42.

and more than usually definite tonality at the end provide the terminal heightening that had by 1609 become indispensable.

If we define terminal heightening broadly enough, it is the most nearly universal pattern in the serial arts. Its enlarged definition would equate it with all means of producing closure, the perception of a work as finished. This sense is produced in the visual arts by suggestions of balance, spatial limitation, and so on; but in serial art it does not depend on symmetry, an attribute of the retrospective mode, so much as on the artist's way of handling a work's last few moments. Closure is first of all a property of the progressive mode. Musical closure at its simplest is the result of a cadential formula followed by silence; if the work is a vocal one, the words of the text may contribute to the sense of finality, too, by a concluding rhyme or by our familiarity with the whole text, as in many liturgical works. The principle of return may make a secondary contribution to the sense of completeness: a modal work was expected to end in the same mode in which it began, and later, as composers explored the artistic possibilities of the diatonic system, it became the rule that the final cadence ought to confirm a work's opening key. Recurrence of an opening theme at the end of a work is a habit that became established only in the seventeenth century, too late for me to include it in the present discussion; but we have seen how recurrent *texture* was being used to the same end as early as 1580. Such retrospective closure is optional; progressive closure by means of an enhanced final cadence is almost inevitable. In polyphonic writing, all available voices are brought in at this point, and there is apt to be increased movement; as Morley puts it, "if your descant should be stirring in any place it should be in the note before the close." [19] We might almost say that climactic form in music is a matter of extending the cadential approach backward to include the entire work.

In the radically segmental variation sets, however, the in-

19. Morley, p. 158.

creased excitement commonly used to signal the final close often expresses itself in the treatment of the whole last variation. Something of this sort must have dictated the involved polyphony that ends Bull's *Walsingham,* and we have already noted that Byrd liked to append a coda (usually a shorter one than in his *Walsingham* set) with one or two rapid runs. The polyphonic last section seems to have lost favor with the younger composers: whereas Byrd uses this method in about one quarter of his variation sets, and Bull, true to his character as a learned composer, shows about the same percentage, Farnaby, Morley, Gibbons, and Tomkins use the polyphonic close rarely if at all. Often the last variation will have rapid passages for the left hand, to take advantage of the greater sonority of the lower range of the instrument; this is a favorite method with Gibbons. Farnaby is more likely to stress the final close either by writing parallel divisions for both hands together, or by writing in a rallentando. The latter device is more often made explicit as our period proceeds; like the growing preference for internal consistency within each variation, the strongly marked closes help to give the works retrospective regularity. In the progressive mode the quickened rhythms that are more and more the rule in the last section produce a quasi-climactic form by means of terminal heightening. This phenomenon has an interesting parallel in Drayton's *Idea* (the revised version of 1619). Here, too, is a radically segmental work, but Drayton carefully arranges the last five sonnets to lead up to and away from the most arresting of the sequence, "Since ther's no hclpc."

This new emphasis on the endings of works is accompanied, as we might expect, by a change in the way works begin. Polyphonic openings in song variations are used very rarely by composers after Byrd, this kind of beginning being reserved for the fantasia, a formal relative of the motet. Farnaby and Tomkins prefer to begin variations with a relatively complex setting, compared with most of Byrd's, but the complexity is a matter of figuration rather than of counterpoint. The taste for more abrupt openings is in keeping with trends in the drama and in the lyric. Preliminary matter, like the explanatory opening scene and the initial posing of a theme in lyric, becomes dispensable. Instead, plays are launched *in medias res,* with lines that sound like the middle of a conversation, with a sudden onrush of brawling characters, with a supposed member of the audience taking the stage in place of the verse-reciting Prologue, and so forth.[20] Very similar in effect is Donne's aggressive lyric strategy in such often-quoted opening lines as "I wonder, by my troth, what thou and I / Did, till we loved"; even the gentler "Sweetest love, I do not go / For weariness of thee" implies that the poem is cutting into an already ongoing situation as surely as does Kent's "I thought the King had more affected the Duke of Albany than Cornwall. . . ." All these opening boundaries suggest a changed feeling about the relation between work and world, an intensified conflict with other possible objects of attention. The listener, reader, or playgoer is no longer expected to be at leisure to attend, or to relish the gradual process of getting under way; his interest must be forcibly demanded, detached by one or another kind of shock tactic from the claims of all the other things that are attracting him. The effort to provoke surprise is a new thing in the 1590s; it is associated with the pattern of expectation and resolution that is the defining mark of climactic form.

20. The instances I have in mind are *The Winter's Tale, The Life of Sir John Oldcastle,* and *The Knight of the Burning Pestle;* others could of course be adduced.

6

The Emergence of Climactic Progression

For the last two chapters we have been concerned principally with certain aspects of segmental forms: the internal organization of segments, the way adjacent segments are related to each other, the arrangement of segments in terms of retrospective form and of the quasi-climactic device that I have called terminal heightening. Heightened endings and abrupt beginnings are psychologically related to intersegmental contrast, but they are by no means exclusive characteristics of segmental works. As we have seen, there was along with increased contrast between segments an increased effort to make the segments cohere. Where a work is basically continuous rather than segmental, the desire for coherence manifests itself in the progressive mode as the preference for a smooth curve of expectation. Since there is no way to box off trends from one another, this smoothness is often a desideratum in works that show segmental organization as well. Spenser's *Fowre Hymnes*, because they have already come into the discussion, are a convenient case in point. Regardless of how we judge his success, Spenser obviously meant the hymns to form a single rising arc in terms of their subjects. Where sections are less clearly demarcated, the smooth curve is easier to achieve, and more likely to appeal to the artist as a means of formal strategy.

The literary type in which we normally expect to find a smooth curve of continuity is narrative, preferably brief narrative without a subplot. In Elizabethan times there was for awhile a vogue for the erotic epyllion, a narrative poem of modest length usually presenting a love story out of classical mythology. The dual prototypes in English of this genre were Marlowe's *Hero and Leander* and Shakespeare's *Venus and*

Adonis. Since the former is unluckily an unfinished work (if we consider only Marlowe's part) or a composite one (if we include Chapman's continuation), *Venus and Adonis* is the more manageable exemplar of the type.[1]

Already in 1593 Shakespeare was using the abrupt opening, with its unprefaced plunge into the action. Where Lodge in *Scillaes Metamorphosis* had given a Chaucerian preamble—the disconsolate poet encounters the subject of his tale by a riverside—and Marlowe had taken time to describe Sestos and Abydos, Shakespeare begins at once with rose-cheeked Adonis and with Venus, who "makes amain unto him, / And like a bold-fac'd suitor 'gins to woo him" in the very first stanza. Once our attention is secured by Venus's and the poet's aggressive methods, there is no further need for sudden surprise. As in an early Haydn sonata, we already know how it all will end, and we are therefore the more willing to let the poet work through to the ending as he will. Shakespeare is very careful neither to let the suspense drop, nor to let it become so compelling as to make us impatient. He leads up to the stages of Venus's pleading in the intervening descriptions, which present the goddess and the unwilling youth in regular alternation. All the narrative is from Venus's point of view, and she does most of the talking; appropriately, then, every interim between her speeches gives a new and more agitated variant of her passion. She makes her first offer thus:

> Being so enrag'd desire doth lend her force
> Courageously to pluck him from his horse.
>   [Ll. 29–30]

Once the mismatched pair are down, "each leaning on their elbows and their hips" (l. 44), physical activity gives way to simile. Venus is like "an empty eagle, sharp by fast . . . de-

1. All line references are to *The New Arden Shakespeare, The Poems,* ed. F. T. Prince. I am also indebted to Douglas Bush, *Mythology and the Renaissance Tradition in English Poetry,* pp. 137–48; Lewis, *English Literature in the Sixteenth Century,* pp. 486–89 and 298–99; and Elizabeth Story Donno, ed., *Elizabethan Minor Epics.*

vouring all in haste"; Adonis like a bird tangled in a net, and "like a dive-dapper, peering through a wave" (ll, 55, 86). One last comparison, of Venus to a thirsty "passenger in summer's heat" (l. 91), brings her desire closer to human experience and makes it less grotesque and more sympathetic, in order to introduce her first extended plea for reciprocal love. The sun plays his part in lines 175–80 and 193–98 as an indication of how the time is passing and as a counterpart of Venus's lust. Frustrated by Adonis's silence, "impatience chokes her pleading tongue" (l. 217); she weeps and fidgets and offers herself in terms so overdone that even Adonis "smiles as in disdain" (l. 241) and manages to escape.

The rising curve of excitement has up to this point been gradual, unperturbed by much activity. Venus's pastoral anatomy is the sort of thing that usually belongs to a moment of consummation, and the danger is that after it our interest will slacken. In order to keep the reader in suspense Shakespeare takes advantage of the one available source of ambiguity, a point on which Ovid is not entirely clear: Adonis just might respond. But since we guess by now that Shakespeare's Adonis probably will not, the action is carried on by the horse, and mutual attraction is fulfilled in a sequence that bears an implied analogy to what Adonis might have done. In this way the other alternative is kept alive without interrupting the pattern of eager wooing versus stony denial.

As soon as the horses have given us sufficient respite and revived our interest in how the wooing will proceed, Venus embarks on the next phase, marked at first by restraint: "Full gently now she takes him by the hand" (l. 361)—which only serves to underline her insistent desire. It would be impossible to have her go through another series of speeches like those at the beginning and still maintain the continuous rise in feeling, so now Adonis replies, to give Venus something to react to. His hard look brings on a reaction indeed: she faints, and through the boy's concern for Venus Shakespeare again teases us with the possibility that his hero may yield. In line with the gradual intensification of ambiguity, this time the hypothetical response

takes place not by analogy with other actors but in the central
situation itself; only Adonis's un-amorous motive frustrates our
hopes, and since the pace is continuing to quicken, those hopes
are aroused again almost at once by the hero's agreement to buy
his freedom with a kiss. "Now quick desire hath caught the
yielding prey" (l. 547); with this slight hint of favor, Venus's
"careless lust stirs up a desperate courage" (l. 556)—but of
course all is to no avail. By this time it is an open question
whether a reader will be more eager for Adonis to stop being
coy or for Venus to let him alone. She bids him farewell, and
the wooing seems to be over, until Adonis mentions the boar,
and down they go again. As in the earlier pseudoconsumma-
tions, "All is imaginary she doth prove" (l. 597); but Shakespeare is not merely playing the same trick over again. Combined with the absurdity is our first forecast of the poem's real
consummation, as Venus describes the boar and proleptically
sees

> An image like thyself, all stain'd with gore;
> Whose blood upon the fresh flowers being shed,
> Doth make them droop with grief and hang the head.
> [Ll. 664–66]

A new source of ambiguity is thus blended with the almost
outworn amorous one. From here on, it will be not Adonis's
possible love but his probable death that is the goal of our
expectation. Through Venus's fears and the increasingly certain hints she receives, we move closer step by step to the climactic vision that confirms her foreboding.

Shakespeare measures our steps with precision. The aim is
not to effect, as does the death of Cordelia, a traumatic shock,
but to shape a graceful arc of feeling. Thus Venus has no
sooner imagined Adonis's mangled body than she veers off into
the delightful account of the hare (with perhaps a submerged
pun, as in Mercutio's "an old hare hoar / Is very good meat in
Lent"). Adonis leaves her, as we knew sooner or later he would;
the goddess passes a restless night "confused in the dark" until
with the new day,

> the gentle lark, weary of rest,
> From his moist cabinet mounts up on high,
> And wakes the morning from whose silver breast
> The sun ariseth in his majesty.
>
> [Ll. 853–56]

How can anything go wrong on a day like this? That, of course, is what the marvelous sunrise is meant to suggest, leaving us the more vulnerable to renewed apprehension when with Venus we hear the far-off sounds of the hunt. Delayed by the underbrush—a forest reality that until now was no part of the poem's scene—"she hears the hounds are at a bay," and shudders, "for now she knows it is no gentle chase" (ll. 877, 883). Tension mounts; standing "in a trembling ecstasy,"

> she spied the hunted boar
> Whose frothy mouth bepainted all with red,
> Like milk and blood being mingled both together,
> A second fear through all her sinews spread.
>
> [Ll. 900–03]

In random flight she comes upon the wounded and dismayed hounds; but instead of what seems the inevitable confirmation of our fears, these sad signs lead to Venus's premature exclamation on death. One of the essential climactic techniques, we should remember, is delay: the longer the line of approach can be drawn without breaking, the more satisfying its reversal will be. Since the climax, like the suggested fulfillment of love, is presented here only in Venus's fancy, her "variable passions" allow her to interpret a huntsman's distant shout as a sign of hope, and to turn aside for a moment, blaming her "rash suspect." The fact that we know her suspicion to be correct does not prevent us from being lulled, too, which gives a convincing slight abruptness to the event that has been so meticulously prepared for:

> The grass stoops not, she treads on it so light,
> And in her haste unfortunately spies
> The foul boar's conquest on her fair delight.
>
> [Ll. 1028–30]

Her reaction is presented seriously enough to carry on the now
descending curve without disharmony, but Venus could hardly
be permitted to lose herself in destructive grief—she is, after
all, traditionally supposed to be a tender and amiable divinity
and is a symbol of exuberant life. The first part of her lament
recalls the dead boy's loveliness as attested by nature's response
to him; the second part outlines prophetically the sorrows that
will hereafter attend on love. Neither part is a bereaved wail
like Venus's complaint to death *before* she discovered Adonis's
body. Shakespeare matter-of-factly introduces the obsequies
with nothing more than a "quoth she," and instead of having
Venus transform Adonis by a show of divine power, simply
lets him melt "like a vapour from her sight" (l. 1166). Flower
in hand, the goddess,

> weary of the world
> Yokes her silver doves, by whose swift aid
> Their mistress mounted through the empty skies
> In her light chariot quickly is convey'd
> Holding their course to Paphos.
>
> [Ll. 1189–93]

For a good many more years, not even Shakespeare was to
realize a smoothly continuous climactic movement in verbal
art with such mastery. The carefully controlled, evenly paced
rise of tension, the muted climax prevented from unbalancing
the poem by transferring some of its potential impact to the
fancied climax that precedes it, the melting away of passion
in the closing stanzas—it is these things, fully as much as the
verbal dexterity and amused tone, that make *Venus and Adonis*
still seem a sophisticated poem. There is not to my knowledge
any other important literary work that shows the same qualities in the same perfection before 1600; for a counterpart we
must look to the madrigals of Thomas Weelkes.

The madrigal had a dual set of possibilities as regards serial
form: the composer could stress its segmentation, as we saw
in chapter 5, or he could treat it so as to bring out its con-

tinuity. A beautiful example of how the smooth curve could be realized musically is Weelkes's well-known madrigal for three voices from the collection of 1597, *Cease sorrows now*.[2] The decision to write for only three voices made it impossible from the outset to indulge in such varieties of polyphonic texture as Wilbye was to use in *Ye that do live in pleasures*. Even though the practice of giving each line of poetic text a different musical phrase results in a certain minimum of segmentation, Weelkes's main emphasis both in texture and in harmony is on closely-knit continuous development. We would say that *Cease sorrows now* is in D minor; Weelkes, however, probably thought in terms of the intervals between pairs of voices, those "flat thirds and sixths" that Morley refers to as being appropriate for a melancholy ditty. In view of Weelkes's extravaganzas of word-painting in *Thule, the period of cosmography* and *As Vesta was from Latmos hill descending*, the homogeneity of *Cease sorrows now* is the more remarkable.

The tonal agreement of sections with each other is the basis on which Weelkes sustains an almost continuous expectancy. This leaning forward at the cadences is not so much a result of overlapping voices as of harmonic structure—a quite "modern" sort of composing in 1597. Because the sense of key is so relatively sure, the cadences on A at bars 8, 12, and 35 have the same effect of temporary pause, of waiting for the next development, that we all recognize in the half-cadence on the dominant at the midway point of so many familiar tunes. The full stop at bar 29 is justified by the words, as is that at bar 52; in the first of these instances D-major harmony continues across the pause, leading through the dominant to the only extended modulation in the work, that is, to the relative major for the line "nor help can stand instead." The second full close is briefer, and immediately leads back into D minor for the

2. Thomas Weelkes, *Madrigals to 3, 4, 5, and 6 Voices* (1597), pp. 29–34. Kerman considers *Cease sorrows now* "clumsy in conception" (*The Elizabethan Madrigal*, p. 226); Fellowes thought it "probably the finest English madrigal for three voices in existence" (*The English Madrigal Composers*, p. 192).

penultimate section, which ends in breathless anticipation on the dominant chord of the sixth. This moment is the decisive one in making *Cease sorrows now* a climactic work; it is the launching point for the often-quoted chromatic ascent on the words "I'll sing my faint farewell."

Towards that phrase everything else is aimed. Especially from about the fifty-third bar the melodic lines tend downward, to make the rising last line more striking; but even earlier, melodic descent is the rule, notably in the setting of "lo care hath now consumed my carcase quite," and "for doleful death." We are not at any point allowed to remain passive, as in the Byrd motet, simply and without anxiety accepting the music while moment by moment it is unfolded to us. On the contrary, the changing harmonies are such as to demand resolution, and we are in suspense until the resolution comes. We are forced to anticipate the next moment, and drawn forward toward the release of the final cadence, in the faith that the ambiguities will at last come out right. Compared with any of the less teleological works that have been discussed earlier, the emotional tension created by the progressive pattern of *Cease sorrows now* is tremendous.

The climactic progression, when it is competently arranged, gives the artist a maximum of control over the emotions of the perceiver. If, as Susanne Langer insists, the strength of art is its imitation of biological rhythms,[3] the strength of climactic order is surely its imitation of the rhythm of sexual experience. The gradually quickening tempo, increasing tension, and sudden release make up a familiar pattern, one of the most compelling in adult human life, and one that is associated also with the great revelatory moments of ecstasy and childbirth. Of course we are moved by art that follows this pattern—it is a vital aspect of what we are, and there is no one to whom it does not matter. Nevertheless, to reduce all its manifestations to mere substitutes for eroticism would be a mistake; the more inclusive concept of climactic form allows us more flexibility

3. Langer, *Feeling and Form*, p. 312 and passim.

and respects the diversity of the pattern's individual realiza-
tions. These may be as various as *Venus and Adonis, The
Alchemist,* and *Othello*; as profound as *King Lear* or as frivo-
lous as Phineas Fletcher's *Venus and Anchises.* Musical examples at this date are most commonly found in solo songs: Dowland's *In darkness let me dwell* uses climactic progression along
with conventionally literal word-setting; the same composer's
Lady if you so spite me builds up to an erotic innuendo; the
climactic scheme lends depth to the religious feeling of Campion's *Never weather-beaten sail.*

The impact of the climactic moment depends upon restraint
and careful pacing of the phases that lead to it. Delay, whether
soft, reluctant, and amorous, or heroic, abiding the ripeness
that is all, is indispensable to the successful maintenance of
the climactic approach. The foreseen end attracts us insistently;
we want—or think we want—to hasten towards it, but haste
is the defeat of the form. If the end is reached without adequate preparation, the intensified feeling that we hope for is
unable to develop fully. Everyone knows of plays and stories
in which too much happens; instead of the single line of power
arching its way from start to finish, a collection of minor surprises serves to keep the work in motion. This is in the main
a literary liability: surprise, the startling reversal, is frequently
mistaken for climax. In order to produce the sudden lift that
belongs to climactic form, a writer will withhold some vital
piece of information and spring it upon us when he has
brought the work's development to a seeming impasse. He
may, in Burke's useful terms, rely on material rather than
formal suspense. Although it naturally does not work very well
in reperusal, this method is not altogether to be frowned upon.
It has given us many good minor works, like *A New Way to
Pay Old Debts* and *Philaster*; but it is a commonplace of criticism that we do not find merely material suspense fully satisfactory in serious contexts. There is no mystery about this: the
potency of the climactic form does not spring from causal relations between events, from looking backward; but from a
teleological progression in which we can and must predict at

least the general character of the outcome with accuracy. Surprise defeats climax when it defeats prediction. Every satisfying form has its unsatisfactory obverse: for climactic form there is crude surprise and contrivance; for the segmental, associational forms there is aimless meandering; for controlled balance there is mechanical regularity. An artist's milieu will not by itself make his work good or bad, but it will influence his choice of what kind of excellence to attempt. Dramatists after Marlowe, poets after Donne, and composers after Morley are likely to attempt climactic form.

On page 70 above, certain categories were offered for types of progression and directional models; but for retrospective form I have hesitated to propose a systematic description. Classification would perhaps be possible, but before any such system is made, we need to have a clearer and more extensive body of evidence than is so far available. What is required if we are to come to understand this mode of our perception is not only psychological experiment, but a greater awareness of the existence and importance of retrospective configurations on the part of those whose skill it is to interpret works of art. Instead of categories, then, I shall propose merely some possible dimensions along which retrospective form may vary. When we compare the *Arcadia* with the *Fowre Hymnes,* there is a difference in the degree to which the retrospective form emerges as an independent pattern. The *Arcadia* in retrospect is still organized in a sequential manner, whereas the *Fowre Hymnes* in retrospect have a regularity of pattern that can exist for us apart from sequence—we could stack the hymns on top of one another or arrange them in this or that visible diagram. It is easier to think this way about some works than about others, and the difference is probably an important one for critical interpretation. Another dimension might be the relevance of the progressive and retrospective modes to each other. I have in mind here an experience that every thoughtful reader or listener must have had: the discovery that repeated perusals of a work disclose new details in the progressive mode that have a bearing on our retrospective view of the work as a whole. The impression of inexhaustible richness that we grow to have of Shakespeare's greatest plays is in some part due to the fact that at every stage of increasing familiarity we are likely to find some verbal or ideational complex, which till then seemed to belong only to local bits of action, fitting together in an unexpected way and forcing us to modify our total impression.

On the other hand, some works contain a greater proportion than others of irreducible material, things that, while they may be convincing as we read along, do not ever become part of the retrospective form. In literature, where the notion of "truth to life" became influential long before the tape recorder made it possible to compose music by combining everyday sounds, the clarity of the retrospective form is often responsible for our sense that a given work represents rather than reports human events. "There is," says Frank Kermode in reference to the novel, "an irreducible minimum of geometry—of humanly needed shape or structure—which finally limits our ability to accept the mimesis of pure contingency." [4] Real life gives a retrospective sense of form only occasionally; when it does, the fact is likely to be remarkable, and to provoke comments that "it's like something out of a book," or "it was providential." Clear retrospective form always implies an artificer. The writer who wants us to mistake his story for a factual report will, whether or not he is conscious of doing so, deliberately blur the retrospective form or refuse to let it take shape. Defoe's *Journal of the Plague Year* is a case in point, as are his novels; there is still some disagreement whether Defoe is properly to be considered a literary artist or a first-class reporter. But speculation is already leading beyond the historical confines of this essay.

4. *The Sense of an Ending*, p. 132.

Bibliography

Editions Cited

Auden, W. H., Kallman, Chester, and Greenberg, Noah, eds. *An Elizabethan Song Book.* New York, 1955. Cited in text as *Anchor.*

Bronson, Bertrand H. *The Traditional Tunes of the Child Ballads.* Vol. 1. Princeton, 1959.

Byrd, William. *The Collected Works of William Byrd.* Edited by Edmund H. Fellowes. 20 vols. London, 1937.

———. *My Ladye Nevells Booke.* Edited by Hilda Andrews. London, 1926.

Donno, Elizabeth Story, ed. *Elizabethan Minor Epics.* New York, 1963.

Dowland, John. *Second Book of Airs,* 1601. Edited by Edmund H. Fellowes. London, 1922.

English Madrigalists, The. Edited by Edmund H. Fellowes and revised by Thurston Dart. London (dates as below).

Vol. 6. John Wilbye, *First Set of Madrigals* (1598). 1966.

Vol. 7. ———. *Second Set of Madrigals* (1609). 1966.

Vol. 9. Thomas Weelkes, *Madrigals to 3, 4, 5 and 6 Voices* (1597). 1966.

Vol. 26. Francis Pilkington, *Second Set of Madrigals and Pastorals* (1624). 1958.

Fuller-Maitland, J. A., and Squire, W. Barclay, eds. *The Fitzwilliam Virginal Book.* 2 vols. New York, 1963. Cited in text as *Fitz.*

Kyd, Thomas. *The Spanish Tragedy.* Edited by Philip Edwards. London, 1959.

Lyly, John. *The Complete Works of John Lyly.* Edited by R. Warwick Bond. 2 vols. Oxford, 1902.

———. *Euphues: The Anatomy of Wit.* Edited by Morris W. Croll. London, 1916.

Morley, Thomas. *A Plain and Easy Introduction to Practical Music,* 1597. Edited by R. Alec Harman. London, 1952.

Musica Britannica (cited in text as *MB*).

Vol. 14. *John Bull: Keyboard Music:* 1. Edited by John Steele and Francis Cameron. London, 1960.

Vol. 19. *John Bull: Keyboard Music*: 2. Edited by Thurston Dart. London, 1963.

Vol. 20. *Orlando Gibbons: Keyboard Music*. Edited by Gerald Hendrie. London, 1962.

Vol. 24. *Giles and Richard Farnaby: Keyboard Music*. Edited by Richard Marlow. London, 1965.

Shakespeare, William. *A New Variorum Edition of Shakespeare*. Vol. 1, *The Sonnets*, edited by Hyder E. Rollins. Philadelphia, 1944.

————.*The Merchant of Venice*. Edited by John R. Brown. New York, 1964.

————. *The Poems*. Edited by F. T. Prince. Cambridge, Mass., 1960.

Sidney Philip. *The Prose Works of Sir Philip Sidney*. Edited by Albert Feuillerat. Cambridge, 1962.

Spenser, Edmund. *The Works of Edmund Spenser, A Variorum Edition*. Vol. 1, *The Minor Poems*, edited by Charles G. Osgood, Henry G. Lotspeich, and Dorothy E. Mason. Baltimore, 1943.

————. *Daphnaida and Other Poems*. Edited by W. L. Renwick. London, 1929.

White, Helen C., Wallerstein, Ruth C., and Quintana, Ricardo, eds. *Seventeenth Century Verse and Prose*, vol. 1. New York, 1951.

INTERPRETIVE WORKS CITED

Abraham, Gerald, ed. *The New Oxford History of Music*. Vol. 4, *The Age of Humanism, 1540–1630*. London, 1968.

Ames, Van Meter. "What is Music?" *Journal of Aesthetics and Art Criticism* 26 (1967): 241–49.

Andrews, H. K. *The Technique of Byrd's Vocal Polyphony*. London, 1966.

Arnheim, Rudolf. *Art and Visual Perception*. Berkeley, 1954.

Barber, C. L. *Shakespeare's Festive Comedy: A Study of Dramatic Form and Its Relation to Social Custom*. Cleveland, 1963.

Bevington, David M. *From "Mankind" to Marlowe: Growth of Structure in the Popular Drama of Tudor England*. Cambridge, Mass., 1962.

Borren, Charles van den. *The Sources of Keyboard Music in England*. London, n.d. [1913].

Bradbrook, M. C. *The Growth and Structure of Elizabethan Comedy*. London, 1955.

Brewer, D. S. " 'The hoole book.' " In *Essays on Malory,* edited by J. A. W. Bennett, pp. 41–63. Oxford, 1963.

Brown, Calvin S. *Music and Literature: A Comparison of the Arts.* Athens, Georgia, 1948.

———. "The Musical Structure of DeQuincey's *Dream-Fugue,*" *Music Quarterly* 24 (1924): 341–50.

Buffum, Imbrie. *Agrippa d'Aubigne's "Les Tragiques": A Study in the Baroque Style in Poetry.* New Haven, 1951.

Buker, Alden. "The Baroque S-T-O-R-M: A Study in the Limits of the Culture-Epoch Theory," *Journal of Aesthetics and Art Criticism* 22 (1964): 303–13.

Burke, Kenneth. *Counter-Statement.* New York, 1931.

———. *The Philosophy of Literary Form.* Baton Rouge, 1941.

Bush, Douglas. *English Literature in the Earlier Seventeenth Century, 1600–1660.* New York, 1945.

———. *Mythology and the Renaissance Tradition in English Poetry.* Rev. ed. New York, 1963.

Cannon, Beekman C., Johnson, Alvin H., and Waite, William G. *The Art of Music.* New York, 1960.

Carpenter, Patricia. "Musical Form Regained," *Journal of Philosophy* 62 (1965): 36–48.

Chardin, Pierre Teilhard de. *The Phenomenon of Man.* Translated by Bernard Wall. New York, 1959.

Clemen, Wolfgang. *English Tragedy before Shakespeare: The Development of Dramatic Speech.* Translated by T. S. Dorsch. London, 1961.

Cohen, John, ed. *Readings in Psychology.* London, 1964.

Colles, H. C. *Voice and Verse: A Study in English Song.* London, 1928.

Crocker, Richard L. *A History of Musical Style.* New York, 1966.

Cruttwell, Patrick. *The Shakespearean Moment and Its Place in the Poetry of the Seventeenth Century.* New York, 1955.

Dart, Thurston. *The Interpretation of Music.* New York, 1963.

Davis, Walter R. "Thematic Unity in the New Arcadia," *Studies in Philology* 57 (1960): 123–43.

Davison, Archibald T., and Apel, Willi, eds. *Historical Anthology of Music. Oriental, Medieval and Renaissance Music.* Rev. ed. Cambridge, Mass., 1949.

Dickinson, George Sherman. "Analogical Relations in Musical Pattern," *Journal of Aesthetics and Art Criticism* 17 (1958): 77–84.

————. *The Pattern of Music.* Poughkeepsie, N.Y., 1939.
Donington, Robert. *The Interpretation of Early Music.* London, 1963.
Doran, Madeleine. *Endeavors of Art: A Study of Form in Elizabethan Drama.* Madison, 1954.
Dürr, Walther. "Rhythm in Music: A Formal Scaffolding of Time." In *The Voices of Time,* edited by J. T. Fraser, pp. 180–200. New York, 1966.
Ehrenzweig, Anton. *The Hidden Order of Art: A Study in the Psychology of the Artistic Imagination.* Berkeley and Los Angeles, 1967.
Ellrodt, Robert. *Neoplatonism in the Poetry of Spenser.* Geneva, 1960.
Evans, Willa McClung. *Ben Jonson and Elizabethan Music.* New York, 1965.
————. *Henry Lawes, Musician and Friend of Poets.* New York, 1941.
Fasel, Ida. "Spatial Form and Spatial Time," *Western Humanities Review* 16 (1962): 223–34.
Fellowes, Edmund H. *The English Madrigal-Composers.* Oxford, 1921.
————. *William Byrd.* London, 1936.
Ferguson, Howard. "Repeats and Final Bars in the Fitzwilliam Virginal Book," *Music and Letters* 43 (1962): 345–50.
Finney, Gretchen Ludke. *Musical Backgrounds for English Literature: 1580–1650.* New Brunswick, 1962.
Francès, Robert. *La Perception de la musique.* Paris, 1958.
Frank, Joseph. "Spatial Form in Modern Literature." In *The Widening Gyre,* pp. 3–62. New Brunswick, 1963.
Frye, Northrop. *Anatomy of Criticism.* Princeton, 1957.
————, ed. *Sound and Poetry. English Institute Essays, 1956.* New York, 1957.
Gaither, Mary. "Literature and the Arts." In *Comparative Literature: Method and Perspective,* edited by Newton P. Stallknecht and Horst Frenz, pp. 153–70. Carbondale, Ill., 1961.
Glyn, Margaret H. *About Elizabethan Virginal Music and Its Composers.* London, 1934.
Gombrich, E. H. "Moment and Movement in Art," *Journal of the Warburg and Courtauld Institute* 27 (1964): 293–306.
Granville-Barker, Harley. *Prefaces to Shakespeare.* Vol. 4. Princeton, 1946.

Grove's Dictionary of Music and Musicians. Edited by Eric Blom. 5th ed. New York, 1960.

Harbage, Alfred. Shakespeare and the Rival Traditions. New York, 1952.

Harman, Alec, and Milner, Anthony. Late Renaissance and Baroque Music (ca. 1525–ca. 1750). Fair Lawn, N.J., 1959.

Hatzfeld, Helmut. Literature through Art: A New Approach to French Literature. New York, 1952.

Hcarnshaw, L. S. "Temporal Integration and Behavior." In Readings in Psychology, edited by John Cohen, pp. 341–53. London, 1964.

Holland, Norman. The Dynamics of Literary Response. New York, 1968.

Hollander, John. The Untuning of the Sky. Princeton, 1961.

Holst, Imogen. Tune. New York, 1900.

Hunter, G. K. John Lyly: The Humanist as Courtier. London, 1962.

Huray, Peter le. Music and the Reformation in England, 1549–1660. London, 1967.

Kastendieck, Miles Merwin. England's Musical Poet, Thomas Campion. New York, 1938.

Kerman, Joseph. "Byrd's Motets: Chronology and Canon," Journal of the American Musicological Society 14 (1961): 359–82.

———. The Elizabethan Madrigal. New York, 1962.

Kermode, Frank. The Sense of an Ending: Studies in the Theory of Fiction. New York, 1967.

Koffka, Kurt. Principles of Gestalt Psychology. New York, 1935.

———. "Problems in the Psychology of Art." In Art: A Bryn Mawr Symposium, pp. 180–273. Bryn Mawr, 1940.

Köhler, Wolfgang. Gestalt Psychology. Rev. ed. New York, 1947.

Kubie, Lawrence. Neurotic Distortion of the Creative Process. Lawrence, Kansas, 1958.

Langer, Susanne K. Feeling and Form. New York, 1953.

Lashley, K. S. "The Problem of Serial Order in Behavior." In Cerebral Mechanisms of Behavior, edited by Lloyd A. Jeffress, pp. 112–36. New York, 1951.

Lefkowitz, Murray. William Lawes. London, 1960.

Lesser, Simon O. Fiction and the Unconscious. Boston, 1957.

Lessing, Gotthold Ephraim. Laocoon. Translated by William A. Steel. London, 1930.

Lewis, C. S. *English Literature in the Sixteenth Century*. Oxford, 1954.

Lindheim, Nancy Rothwax. "Sidney's *Arcadia*, Book II: Retrospective Narrative," *Studies in Philology* 64 (1967): 159–86.

Lord, Catherine. "Aesthetic Unity," *Journal of Philosophy* 58 (1961): 321–27.

———. "Unity with Impunity," *Journal of Aesthetics and Art Criticism* 26 (1967): 103–06.

Lovejoy, Arthur O. *Essays in the History of Ideas*. New York, 1960.

Margolis, Joseph. "Aesthetic Perception," *Journal of Aesthetics and Art Criticism* 19 (1960): 209–13.

Maritain, Jacques. *Creative Intuition in Art and Poetry*. Cleveland, 1954.

Mark, James. "The Uses of the Term 'Baroque,' " *Modern Language Review* 33 (1938): 547–63.

Mellers, Wilfrid. *Harmonious Meeting: A Study of the Relationship between English Music, Poetry, and Theatre, c. 1600–1900*. London, 1965.

———. "John Bull and English Keyboard Music," *Music Quarterly* 40 (1954): 364–82 and 548–71.

———. "Words and Music in Elizabethan England." In *The Age of Shakespeare*, edited by Boris Ford, pp. 386–415. Baltimore, 1964.

Meyer, Ernst H. *English Chamber Music*. London, 1946.

Meyer, Leonard B. *Emotion and Meaning in Music*. Chicago, 1956.

———. *Music, the Arts, and Ideas: Patterns and Predictions in Twentieth-Century Culture*. Chicago, 1967.

Miller, Hugh M. "John Bull's Organ Works," *Music and Letters* 28 (1947): 25–35.

Morrison, Claudia C. *Freud and the Critic: The Early Use of Depth Psychology in Literary Criticism*. Chapel Hill, 1968.

Myrick, Kenneth. *Sir Philip Sydney as a Literary Craftsman*. Lincoln, Neb., 1965.

Nelson, Lowry, Jr. "The Rhetoric of Ineffability: Toward a Definition of Mystical Poetry," *Comparative Literature* 8 (1956): 323–36.

Nelson, Robert U. *The Technique of Variation: A Study of the Instrumental Variation from Antonio de Cabezón to Max Reger*. Berkeley and Los Angeles, 1948.

Nelson, William. *The Poetry of Edmund Spenser*. New York, 1963.

Obler, Paul. "Psychology and Literary Criticism: A Summary and Critique," *Literature and Psychology* 8 (1958): 50–59.

Oldfield, R. C. "Experiment in Psychology—A Centenary and an Outlook." In *Readings in Psychology,* edited by John Cohen, pp. 29–47. London, 1964.

Pattison, Bruce. *Music and Poetry of the English Renaissance.* London, 1948.

Peckham, Morse. *Man's Rage for Chaos: Biology, Behavior, and the Arts.* Philadelphia, 1965.

Pepper, Stephen C. *The Basis of Criticism in the Arts.* Cambridge, Mass., 1946.

Petri, Horst. *Literatur und musik: form- und struktur-parallelen.* Göttingen, 1964.

Phillips, James E. "Poetry and Music in the Seventeenth Century." In *Music and Literature, Clark Library Seminar.* Los Angeles, 1953.

Pratt, Carroll C. "The Perception of Art," *Journal of Aesthetics and Art Criticism* 23 (1964): 57–62.

Reese, Gustave. *Music in the Renaissance.* Rev. ed. New York, 1954.

Révész, Géza. *Introduction to the Psychology of Music.* Translated by G. I. C. de Courcy. Norman, Okla., 1953.

Richards, I. A. *Practical Criticism.* New York, 1928.

Roberts, Donald Ramsay. "The Music of Milton," *Philological Quarterly* 26 (1947): 328–44.

Roche, Thomas P., Jr. *The Kindly Flame.* Princeton, 1964.

Rosenblatt, Louise M. "Towards a Transactional Theory of Reading," *Journal of Reading Behavior* 1 (1969): 31–50.

Seashore, Carl E. *Psychology of Music.* New York, 1938.

Smith, Barbara H. *Poetic Closure: A Study of How Poems End.* Chicago, 1968.

Spurgeon, Caroline F. E. *Shakespeare's Imagery and What It Tells Us.* Cambridge, 1965.

Stambaugh, Joan. "Music as a Temporal Form," *Journal of Philosophy* 61 (1964): 265–80.

Stevens, Denis. *The Mulliner Book: A Commentary.* London, 1952.

———. *Thomas Tomkins, 1572–1656.* New York, 1967.

———. *Tudor Church Music.* Rev. ed. New York, 1966.

Stevens, John. "The Elizabethan Madrigal," *Essays and Studies by Members of the English Association,* n.s. 11 (1958): 17–37.

———. *Music and Poetry in the Early Tudor Court.* London, 1961.

Sutton, Walter. "The Literary Image and the Reader: A Consideration of the Theory of Spatial Form," *Journal of Aesthetics and Art Criticism* 16 (1957): 112–23.

Sypher, Wylie. *Four Stages of Renaissance Style*. New York, 1955.
Tovey, Donald Francis. *The Forms of Music*. Cleveland, 1956.
Ulrich, Homer. *Chamber Music*. 2d ed. New York, 1966.
Wellek, Albert. "The Relationship between Music and Poetry," *Journal of Aesthetics and Art Criticism* 21 (1962): 149–56.
Wellek, René. *Concepts of Criticism*. Edited by Stephen G. Nichols, Jr. New Haven, 1963.
———. "The Parallelism between Literature and the Arts," In *English Institute Annual, 1941*, pp. 29–63. New York, 1942.
Welsford, Enid. *Spenser: Fowre Hymnes, Epithalamion; A Study of Edmund Spenser's Doctrine of Love*. Oxford, 1967.
Whaler, James. *Counterpoint and Symbol: An Inquiry into the Rhythm of Milton's Epic Style*. Copenhagen, 1956.
Wilson, Katharine M. "The Correlation of Poetry with Music," *British Journal of Psychology* 14 (1923): 206–17.
Wölfflin, Heinrich. *Principles of Art History: The Problem of the Development of Style in Later Art*. Translated by M. D. Hottinger. New York, 1932.
Zuckerkandl, Victor. *Sound and Symbol: Music and the External World*. Translated by Willard R. Trask. New York, 1956.

Selected Discography

The following list has two parts. First is a key to various available recordings of Elizabethan music, arranged alphabetically by record number. Second is a list of musical works cited in my text, with the number of one or more recordings on which the work can be heard. The criterion for selection of these records is whether they contain some work I have mentioned in the text. Where there was a choice of several records, I have tried to include those I consider the best, but excellence of performance has necessarily been a secondary consideration. Some works that have a place in my text are not to my knowledge available on records, e.g. the two sets of *Walsingham* variations.

KEY TO RECORD NUMBERS

5896	London: Peter Pears and Julian Bream. *Recital of Lute Songs.*
32160171	Odyssey: Russell Oberlin, New York Pro Musica. *An Evening of Elizabethan Verse and Its Music.*
ARC 3053	DGG Archive: Deller Consort, Consort of Viols of the Schola Cantorum Basilensis. *Orlando Gibbons: Anthems, Madrigals, and Fantasies.*
BC 1298	Epic: Igor Kipnis. *English Harpsichord Music.*
BG 553	Bach Guild: Deller Consort. *The English Madrigal School, vol. 1.*
BG 578	Bach Guild: Deller Consort. *The English Madrigal School. Vol. 4, Madrigals of John Wilbye.*
CE 31005	Candide: The Purcell Consort of Voices and the Jaye Consort of Viols, conducted by Grayston Burgess. *English Secular Music of the Late Renaissance.*

CPT 520   Counterpoint: The New York Pro Musica.
              Thomas Morley: Elizabethan Madrigals.
CPT 5540   Counterpoint: The New York Pro Musica.
              Children's Songs of Shakespeare's Time.
DD 9406   Decca: Russell Oberlin, Bethany Beardslee,
              Paul Maynard, and the New York Pro Musica.
              *Elizabethan and Jacobean Ayres, Madrigals,
              and Dances.*
DL 79415   Decca: Paul Maynard and the New York Pro
              Musica. *Instrumental Music from the Courts
              of Queen Elizabeth and King James.*
DL 79434   Decca: Edward Smith and the New York Pro
              Musica. *The Kynge's Musicke.*
EA 34   Expériences Anonymes: Russell Oberlin and
              Joseph Iadone. *John Dowland: Lute Songs.*
HB 73010   Nonesuch: Dolmetsch Consort and other in-
              strumentalists and singers conducted by Au-
              gust Wenzinger. *Music of Shakespeare's Time.*
HCR-ST-7015   Dover: Blanche Winogron. *The Fitzwilliam
              Virginal Book.*
LLST 7156   Lyrichord: The Saltire Singers. *William Byrd:
              Madrigals, Motets, and Anthems.*
OL 50076   London L'Oiseau-Lyre: Thurston Dart. *Mas-
              ters of Early English Keyboard Music, 2: Wil-
              liam Byrd and Thomas Tomkins.*
OL 50131   London L'Oiseau-Lyre: Thurston Dart. *Mas-
              ters of Early English Keyboard Music, 4: Or-
              lando Gibbons and Giles Farnaby.*
SVBX 572   Vox: Joseph Payne. *A Comprehensive Selec-
              tion from the Fitzwilliam Virginal Book.*
TV 34017S   Turnabout: The Purcell Consort of Voices
              and the Jaye Consort of Viols. *Music of the
              High Renaissance in England.*
TV 34200   Turnabout: Sylvia Kind. *English Tone Paint-
              ings, Toccatas, and Dances.*
ZRG 5316   Argo: The Choir of King's College, Cam-

bridge, conducted by David Willcocks. *John Taverner: Tudor Church Music.*

RECORDINGS OF MUSICAL WORKS CITED

Anonymous. *Barafostus' Dreame.* HCR-ST-7015.

Anonymous. *Watkins Ale.* SVBX 572.

Bull, John. *The Spanish Pavan.* HCT-ST-7015.

Byrd, William. *The Carman's Whistle.* TV 34200, SVBX 572.

——. *Civitas sancti tui.* LLST 7156.

——. *Lord Willoughby's Welcome Home.* DL 79415, OL 50076.

——. *Monsieur's Alman.* HCR-ST-7015, SVBX 572.

——. *O Mistress Mine.* HB 73010, DL 79434.

——. *Pavan and Galliard in A re.* DL 9406.

——. *Pavan and Galliard* (first). OL 50076.

——. *Sellinger's Round.* HB 73010.

——, *Wolsey's Wild.* BC 1298, SVBX 572.

Campion, Thomas. *Fair, if you expect admiring.* 5896.

——. *Jack and Jone they think no ill.* CPT 5540.

——. *Never weather-beaten sail.* HB 73010.

Dowland, John. *Flow my tears.* EA 34, DL 9406.

——. *If my complaints.* 5896.

——. *In darkness let me dwell.* EA 34, 32160171.

——. *Lady, if you so spite me.* EA 34, DL 9406.

Farnaby, Giles. *Rosasolis.* DL 79434, OL 50131.

——. *Wooddy-Cock.* HCR-ST-7015.

Gibbons, Orlando. *What is our life.* ARC 3053, 32160171.

Jones, Robert. *Sweet, if you like and love me still.* 32160171.

Morley, Thomas. *Miraculous love's wounding.* CPT 520.

Pilkington, Francis. *Rest, sweet nymphs.* 5896, CPT 5540.

Taverner, John. *Mass "The Western Wind."* ZRG 5316.

Weelkes, Thomas. *As Vesta was from Latmos hill descending.* TV 34017S.

——. *Cease sorrows now.* BG 553.

——. *Thule, the period of cosmography.* CE 31005.

Wilbye, John. *Happy, oh happy he.* BG 578.

——. *Thus saith my Cloris bright.* BG 578.

——. *Ye that do live in pleasures.* BG 578.

Index

Pages showing music examples are listed in italics.